Caleb R. L. Wall, Peter P. Mollinga (Eds.)

Fieldwork in Difficult Environments

# ZEF Development Studies

edited by

Solvay Gerke and Hans-Dieter Evers

Volume 7

Center for Development Research (ZEF)
University of Bonn
www.zef.de

LIT

# Fieldwork in Difficult Environments

## Methodology as Boundary Work in Development Research

edited by

## Caleb R. L. Wall and Peter P. Mollinga

LIT

**Bibliographic information published by the Deutsche Nationalbibliothek**
The Deutsche Nationalbibliothek lists this publication in the Deutsche
Nationalbibliografie; detailed bibliographic data are available in the Internet at
http://dnb.d-nb.de.

ISBN 978-3-03735-909-9 (Schweiz)
ISBN 978-3-8258-1282-9 (Deutschland)

**A catalogue record for this book is available from the British Library**

© LIT VERLAG GmbH & Co. KG Wien,
Zweigniederlassung Zürich  2008
Dufourstr. 31
CH-8008 Zürich
Tel. +41 (0) 44-251 75 05
Fax +41 (0) 44-251 75 06
e-Mail: zuerich@lit-verlag.ch
http://www.lit-verlag.ch

LIT VERLAG Dr. W. Hopf
Berlin 2008
Auslieferung/Verlagskontakt:
Fresnostr. 2
D-48159 Münster
Tel. +49 (0)251–62 03 20
Fax +49 (0)251–23 19 72
e-Mail: lit@lit-verlag.de
http://www.lit-verlag.de

**Auslieferung:**
Schweiz/Österreich: Medienlogistik Pichler-ÖBZ GmbH & Co KG
IZ-NÖ, Süd, Straße 1, Objekt 34, A-2355 Wiener Neudorf
Tel. +43 (0) 2236/63 535 - 290, Fax +43 (0) 2236/63 535 - 243, e-Mail: mlo@medien-logistik.at
Deutschland: LIT Verlag Fresnostr. 2, D-48159 Münster
Tel. +49 (0) 2 51/620 32 - 22, Fax +49 (0) 2 51/922 60 99, e-Mail: vertrieb@lit-verlag.de

Distributed in the UK by: Global Book Marketing, 99B Wallis Rd, London, E9 5LN
Phone: +44 (0) 20 8533 5800 – Fax: +44 (0) 1600 775 663
http://www.centralbooks.co.uk/acatalog/search.html

Distributed in North America by:

**Transaction Publishers**
New Brunswick (U.S.A.) and London (U.K.)

Transaction Publishers
Rutgers University
35 Berrue Circle
Piscataway, NJ 08854

Phone: +1 (732) 445 - 2280
Fax: + 1 (732) 445 - 3138
for orders (U. S. only):
toll free (888) 999 - 6778
e-mail:
orders@transactionspub.com

# Contents

*List of boxes*                                                                 iii

*List of tables*                                                                iii

*List of maps*                                                                  iii

*List of figures*                                                               iii

*About the authors*                                                             iv


1.    Field Research Methodology as Boundary Work. An introduction

    *Peter P. Mollinga*                                                           1


2.    Losing My Illusions. Methodological dreams and reality in local governance research in the Amu Darya borderlands

    *Bernd Kuzmits*                                                              19


3.    Positioning "Security" and Securing One's Position. The researcher's role in investigating "security" in Kyrgyzstan

    *Claire Wilkinson*                                                           43


4.    Cultivating Fields of Knowledge. The problem of knowledge transfer in field research on land use in Burkina Faso

    *Katrin Gleisberg*                                                           69

5. The Best of Both Worlds. Integrating quantitative and qualitative approaches in research on forest management in Indonesia

*Charles Palmer*                                                                              83


6. Knowledge Resources (Yet) Untapped. The challenge of finding one's place in an interdisciplinary water research project on the Volta River basin, West Africa.

*Irit Eguavoen*                                                                              111


7. Working in Fields as Fieldwork. *Khaskar*, participant observation and the *tamorka* as ways to access local knowledge in rural Uzbekistan.

*Caleb Wall*                                                                                 137


8. Authoritarianism, Validity, and Security. Researching water distribution in Khorezm, Uzbekistan.

*G.J.A. Veldwisch*                                                                           161

# Boxes

1.1     Research topics of the PhD projects reported on in this volume    2

# Tables

2.1     Initial set of methods    26

7.1     Gendered specialisation in household silk worm production    155

8.1     Three levels of methodology as applied in the research    164

# Maps

2.1     First Field Trip    29

2.2     Second Field Trip    30

2.3     Third Field Trip    30

# Figures

6.1     A holistic approach to household water    115

6.2     Task sharing in the project (phase I and phase II)    119

# About the authors

*Irit Eguavoen* continued working at ZEF as Senior Researcher after graduating from its doctoral program in 2007. Her present focus is on natural resources management, youth and conflict in Africa. Email: irit.eguavoen@hotmail.com

*Katrin Gleisberg* is a PhD candidate at ZEF. Her thesis explores drivers and impacts of land use and land cover change on rural livelihoods in Burkina Faso. Email: katrin.zitzmann@uni-bonn.de

*Bernd Kuzmits* is Research Fellow at ZEF since 2003. He works on cross-border interactions for the project 'Local Governance and Statehood in the Amu Darya Border Region' funded by the Volkswagen Foundation. Email: bkuzmits@uni-bonn.de

*Peter P. Mollinga* is Senior Researcher 'Natural Resources and Social Dynamics' at ZEF since 2004. He works on water, politics and development, particularly in Asia. Email: pmollinga@hotmail.com

*Charles Palmer* is Senior Researcher in Environmental and Resource Economics at the Swiss Federal Institute of Technology (ETH), Zürich, Switzerland. He completed his PhD in Agricultural Economics at ZEF in 2005. Email: charles.palmer@env.ethz.ch

*Gert Jan Veldwisch* has written his PhD thesis on water distribution processes in Uzbekistan while being based at ZEF. Currently he works as a Post-Doctoral Fellow for CIAT in Mozambique. Email: veldwisch@gmail.com

*Caleb R.L. Wall* graduated from ZEF with a PhD in 2006 and is a freelance consultant based in Italy consulting for ZEF Consult a.o.. He currently works in Kazakhstan, Russia and increasingly in Eastern and Southern Africa. Email: caleb.wall@gmail.com

***Claire Wilkinson*** is a PhD candidate at the Centre for Russian & East European Studies, University of Birmingham, UK. Her thesis examines group identities and perceptions of security threats in Kyrgyzstan. Email: cxwilkinson@googlemail.com

# 1

# *Field Research Methodology as Boundary Work*

## An introduction

### Peter P. Mollinga

*"Conducting research in the field is rarely a straight-forward business. The most careful planning can mean little once the researcher moves into the field and encounters the real world." (Willis, 2005)*

In this volume PhD researchers speak about difficulties they have encountered in their field research. They document these and reflect on them. The chapters are personal accounts – quite deliberately. There is no scarcity of textbooks on field research methodology and all the PhD research reported on in this volume has made use of that. The textbooks have helped the PhD researchers to design coherent methodological approaches to answer their research questions. Through the method of personal accounts we can bring to light the gap between textbook theory and method in practice. In a way, implementing a methodological approach in the field is a process of negotiation: negotiation of the setting – the enabling and constraining societal conditions, negotiation of ethical principles and political standpoints, negotiation of institutional and communication boundaries in research projects, negotiation of cultural chasms, and so forth. None of these issues are new as such. Some of them are treated extensively in the literature on field research methodology. For instance, anthropology has a literature on field experience and self reflection which enjoys great popularity and shows clearly the divergence between what was planned and then experienced, most (in)famously in Malinowski´s diaries.[1] Nevertheless, there usually is a degree of 'sanitization'[2] in the presentation of methodological difficulty and its consequences in the final product of the PhD thesis, as there is, for that matter, in the publications of post-PhD researchers. Through the medium of personal accounts of methodological struggles we aim to raise a number of issues that are usually not so openly talked, or rather written about.

All the research reported on in this volume falls in the category of 'development research'. The research is located in developing and transition countries and all projects have 'development' as part of their subject matter in one way or the other. Box 1.1 lists the topics of the research projects reported on.

---

**Box 1.1: Research topics of the PhD projects reported on in this volume**

- Cross-border interactions and their effects on local governance in the Amu Darya borderlands (Afghanistan, Tajikistan, Uzbekistan) *(Bernd Kuzmits)*
- Societal identities and security in Kyrgyzstan *(Claire Wilkinson)*
- Assessing land use and land cover change in south-western Burkina Faso: a multi-agent approach *(Katrin Gleisberg)*.
- Household water management, water rights and institutional change in Northern Ghana *(Irit Eguavoen)*
- Forest management practices, timber trade and decentralisation in Indonesia *(Charles Palmer)*
- Agricultural knowledge systems in rural Uzbekistan *(Caleb Wall)*
- Irrigation water management and agrarian transformation in Khorezm province, Uzbekistan *(G.J.A. Veldwisch)*

---

Most of the research has been conducted through ZEF, the Center for Development Research at Bonn University, Germany. This brings with it certain features. The projects are conventional PhD projects in the sense that they are individual pieces of research, based on a research proposal prepared 'at home' in the Center, with a fieldwork period of about a year, and a writing period of one to one and a half years. The products, PhD theses or sets of articles, were or will be evaluated in standard academic fashion. What further specifically characterises the projects is that there is a strong tendency towards interdisciplinarity, related to the desire to understand development issues comprehensively. Quite a few of the PhD projects were part of larger collaborative and interdisciplinary research projects. Much of the research reported is situated in difficult environments in the sense of difficult political environments – like Uzbekistan and Afghanistan. This publication started with the idea to discuss the difficulties of research in such situations in particular, but in the process of putting it together the understanding of 'difficult environments' broadened. Field research in difficult political environments brings to light certain methodological difficulties very prominently, but in the final analysis they are part of development research of all varieties. The citation at the top of this chapter is taken from a paper discussing the difficulties of doing field research among ex-prisoners in Australia.

The metaphor to bring the different accounts in the volume together is that of the 'boundary work' that is involved in doing field research. The term is taken from the literature on sustainability science (Cash et al., 2003). Sustainability science is characterised by collaborative, problem solving oriented and interdisciplinary research projects. The larger research projects of ZEF that provide the context of much of the research reported on in this volume are of this nature.

Sustainability science type of research generates the need for many kinds of boundary work. The focus of discussion in Cash et al. (2003) is the research-policy boundary: the specific efforts required to make scientific research useful for decision-making in the policy domain, by enhancing its salience and legitimacy in addition to its credibility, and negotiate the trade-offs involved. At this interface between research and policy active communication, translation and mediation processes are required, for which effective systems need to be set up. These are the institutional arrangements, procedures and norms of boundary work.

The notion can be expanded to other frontiers also. Mollinga (forthcoming) uses the notion of 'boundary crossing' as a metaphor for interdisciplinarity in general.[3] The paper argues that problem solving oriented interdisciplinary (and transdisciplinary) research on natural resources management generates the following three types of work.[4]

1.  The development of boundary concepts (to be able to think multi-dimensionality and complexity).

2.  The design of boundary objects (the devices to help take decisions at the interface of different domains and life worlds).

3.  The crafting of boundary settings (the internal and external institutional arrangements of research projects).

The research-policy interface discussed by Cash et al. is characterised by the development of a great many boundary objects in the form of decision support systems, often to operationalise for decision-making integrative policy boundary concepts like 'sustainability' and 'human development'. Such concepts want to capture complex situations and objectives 'comprehensively', and require devices through which multiple dimensions can be assessed and weighted.[5] An example of (constraining) boundary settings relevant to the papers in this volume, is the disciplinarity/ interdisciplinarity incentive problem. One contradiction facing PhD researchers working in the larger collaborative projects is that of contradictory incentives as regards that collaboration, including mixed messages on it from their guides. Being part of collaborative projects they are asked to invest time not only in their own PhD project but also in project activities, and adapt their research design and data collection to the requirements of the project to a certain degree. At the same time most PhD students have to defend their PhD thesis in a disciplinary university setting as individuals. In general in academia, credits for disciplinary work are higher than for interdisciplinary endeavour (the latter is considered science of a lesser kind by many) and the transaction costs of interdisciplinary research are higher. These issues are well known from the literature on interdisciplinarity (see for instance Klein, 1990, 1996) and are not repeated in this volume (but see the chapter by Eguavoen). A process of 'professionalising' the boundary management inherent to interdisciplinary research is ongoing (see for instance Pohl and Hirsch-Hadorn, 2007; Stoll-Kleemann and Pohl, 2007). Going by the ZEF experience, this boundary may indeed be becoming less of a problem than it was. Employment-wise interdisciplinary skills seem to be in high demand in the broader domain of development research and practice.

Another boundary to manage, and the main subject of this volume, is that between the PhD researcher and his/her (difficult) environment. Development field research methodology in difficult environments has aspects of all three types of boundary crossing work mentioned above. It requires a flexible conceptual stance and related pragmatism as regards methodological philosophy and choice; it may require the design of specific boundary objects, as evident for example in mapping techniques for participatory research; and it requires strategic shaping of the social relations of data collection. The need for 'flexibility' much referred to in textbooks on field research methodology[6] thus has at least three dimensions: a philosophical, a technical, and a social. These play out in individual research projects in a variety of ways, around specific issues. The boundaries that need to be crossed, negotiated and managed are discussed in this volume under four headings, with no claim made that this is an exhaustive list of issues.

1. Cultural difference

2. Methodological style and the scale level of research

3. Communication and interaction in collaborative research

4. The political and ethical legitimacy of research

The general message of the volume is that these issues are not just 'problems' to 'overcome' but features that continue to present themselves during development field research and need to be (constantly) negotiated and managed. The notion of methodology as boundary work and boundary management thus is also a critique of static conceptions of methodological rigour and 'methodolatry' (O'Leary, 2004:2; Janesick, 1994), in favour of an understanding that choice and deployment of methodology is an ongoing, reflexive process. The practical challenge is how to be flexible and adaptive while maintaining rigour, that is, while assuring validity and coverage of data collection. As O'Leary states "[Research] is a creative and strategic process that involves constantly assessing, reassessing, and making decisions about the best possible means for obtaining trustworthy information, carrying out appropriate analysis, and drawing credible conclusions." (O'Leary, 2004:1) Her advice to 'budding researchers' is that "[t]he perspectives you will adopt and the methods you will use need to be as fluid, flexible and eclectic as is necessary to answer the questions posed." (ibid.:2) This position is well in line with the 'problem solving orientation' of sustainability science, and therefore not only relevant for newly starting researchers.

The remainder of this introductory chapter discusses the methodological boundary experiences of the research reported in subsequent chapters.

In chapter 2 Kuzmits describes how he lost his methodological illusions while conducting field research as part of a project on local governance in three countries with a common but also separate history in the Amu Darya river basin: Afghanistan, Uzbekistan, and Tajikistan. His research attempts to investigate cross-border interactions in this region, to be taken literally here as the processes happening across the national boundaries of these three countries. The chapter is a strong statement on the gap between methodological theory and practice that may exist in development research.

Part of Kuzmits' (admittedly self-created) frustration is that he is unable to do research following the methodological principles of his discipline, political science. This is caused by his 'vague role' within the research project he is part of, as well as the fluidity of the situation on the ground in the research area, which makes the identification of (relatively stable) causal mechanisms operative in cross-border processes more than a little hazardous. The lesson he learns is to be modest in output ambitions, to adopt an 'observe and describe' approach to research, and to be content "with the aim to pose the right questions". This seems a rather sane attitude. Kuzmits nicely describes his systematically designed methodology of different research techniques for different components of his envisaged research, and how this fares when confronted with field reality. Many factors come into play: the political sensitivity of working in border areas, the far greater than anticipated diversity of cross-border interactions, bureaucratic complications and delays, logistical difficulties, time constraints and others. As a result "the colourful bouquet of methods withered to little more than the basic skills of direct observation and informal conversation." In his case research literally became a journey, through three border areas, and his accounts seems to suggest that it is experience of the journeying itself that provides a lot of the insights gained.

Wilkinson, also a political scientist, in chapter 3 reports a similar struggle with theory (the Copenhagen school of security studies). Her paper relates how in a situation of rapid socio-political transformation in Kyrgyzstan it made more sense to her to 'ignore the discipline and concentrate on "being there"', resorting to ethnographic method, while critically interrogating and problematising theoretical constructs rather than operationalising them. In her case this led to fundamental questions about the theme and topic of the research itself: the meaning of 'security', and to equally fundamental questions about the role of the researcher's identity in constructing data and analysis.

Though it is tempting to designate Kuzmits' and Wilkinson's research as exceptional cases, as exceedingly difficult research given the region and problematic it seeks to work on, this would be too strong a conclusion. The research region and topic certainly have features that make the research inherently difficult, but the case is perhaps more a somewhat strong case of a normal development research situation than an exception. After all, the ongoing social transformation that we call development is inherently a non-linear, contested and complex process, and therefore often without much predictability and stability. Illusions should, indeed, be discarded, while the reality of field research methodology should be squarely addressed as being, in Wilkinson's words, disordered, confusing, illogical and serendipitous. Methodologies may be vulnerable, as Kuzmits notes, due to the complexity and sensitivity of the situation investigated, but that is, in some respects, exactly where the need for development research springs from.

Subsequent chapters deal with more specific aspects of field research methodology. I describe the main contributions they make under the four headings listed above. The order of inclusion of the papers in the volume roughly follows the order of presentation below – roughly because several papers contribute to more than one aspect.

## Cultural difference

Having to deal with cultural difference in conducting field research is probably the most well-known boundary to negotiate in development studies, certainly in those of the anthropological and sociological kind. Very practical aspects of that are the issues of speaking the language of the community in which the research takes place, including learning local terminology/ concepts, and adapting one's personal behaviour to local norms and customs. In this volume these issues are prominently discussed in the contributions by Wilkinson and Gleisberg. Kuzmits in chapter 2 also discusses a number of cultural aspects in his section on 'anecdotal experiences from the field'.

Wilkinson's account (chapter 3) of dealing with cultural difference focuses on the identity and personality of the researcher, how that can be actively managed, or not, and how it influences data collected. Rather than 'blending in' and 'going native' she decided to remain a relative outsider, as she found this personally more comfortable. Her account suggests that categories like 'blending in' as a methodological ideal are not very helpful in the first place. Field research involves dealing with multiple identities and personalities of a diversity of respondents, while the researcher her/himself also is a plurality of selves – being male or female, gay or heterosexual, married or unmarried, western or not, young or old, a researcher or not, and so forth. All of these (can) shape the research, at multiple levels of interpretation. Wilkinson suggests that reflexive engagement with this human aspect of research should be explicitly addressed in the presentation of research findings rather than being swept under the carpet.

The issue that Gleisberg discusses (chapter 4) is also different from an individual having to 'blend into' the society that is the subject of inquiry. She discusses the problems associated with the employment of local residents as survey interviewers and her supervision of two local students, revolving around the issue of perspective sharing and communication. She notes that textbooks recommend the hiring of professional interviewers from the same ethnic group as the researched community, but in practice she found it diffi- cult to find such people in a context where "the number of ethnic groups and languages is almost uncountable" and the illiteracy rate is around 80%. Though the problems described in Gleisberg's chapter as regards conducting surveys with the aid of locally recruited assistants are well known, and 'stan- dard' in a certain respect, how these can be solved is a highly non-standard because context specific matter, for which PhD researchers, and one guesses others as well, are usually poorly prepared. Gleisberg describes the kind of management skills required to successfully coordinate a research team, and the difficulty of performing the multiple roles of student oneself, while simul- taneously being colleague, teacher and employer also.[7] There are undoubtedly negative trade-offs for the quality of the data collected related to the prob- lems as described in the paper, though the experience itself also enhances insight into the society researched. The negative tradeoffs are as difficult to avoid as they are to assess. The simple process of conducting a survey turns out to be a complex intersection of a number of broader structures and proc- esses, including different learning cultures, multiplicity of roles, and the post- colonial condition defining the research taking place as such, as well as creat- ing certain behavioural expectations on either side. The metaphor Gleisberg uses to describe the boundary work she was involved in is that of 'cultivating fields of knowledge', meaning to convey the process of finding pragmatic solutions for knowledge disparities in a complex cultural situation.

## Methodological style and the scale level of research

One of the most lasting controversies in discussions on research methodol- ogy is that about the relative merits of quantitative and qualitative research methods. This boundary is explored in Palmer's paper (chapter 5) for re- search on forest management in Indonesia. Like many others, Palmer con- cludes that the preferred route is not either/or but building on the strengths of both, finding the 'appropriate mix'. The paper identifies several of the reasons why this 'win-win option' is not a route frequently taken. One obser- vation he makes is that while competition among scientists may enhance the quality of research, it also makes collaboration more difficult. There is, thus, an incentives problem and an organisational problem in achieving collabora- tion. One could add to this that there is also a cultural problem, as disciplines, or other constituencies advocating quantitative or qualitative methods, tend to behave as 'tribes', that is, a number of behavioural traits and territorialism that has very little to do with questions of theory and methodology.

How strongly internalised cultural images are of different disciplines shows when in teaching the new batch of PhD students at ZEF about inter-disciplinarity I show three pictures to the group, and state one is a natural scientist, one an economist, and one a sociologist/anthropologist, and ask them to vote who is who. There is overwhelming agreement, with each picture catching about 90% of the vote for a particular discipline, no matter how many nationalities are in the room. I then subsequently inform the students that I have no idea who these people are, not even whether they are academics, and that these pictures were taken from the series of pictures downloaded from the internet by a research assistant and from which I selected three that I though looked like a natural scientist, an economist and a sociologist. Apparently we associate certain 'looks' with certain disciplines – the broader argument being that disciplines are indeed cultures, and, so it seems, transnational cultures (Becher, 1989).

Associated with the quantitative/qualitative divide is often the issue of scale. As Palmer suggests, quantitative, statistical studies tend to be located at higher, say regional, scale levels than qualitative studies, which are often local level case studies. The relationship is not a necessary relationship – research at the global level may well be qualitative, while village level research may well be quantitative – but the association commonly occurs in practice, and is certainly part of the dominant understanding of the quantitative vs. qualitative method issue. One way forward would thus be to disconnect 'quantitative' and 'qualitative' from characteristics often, but too easily associated with it, like that of scale. Palmer's paper also shows that when a conscious effort is made to combine quantitative and qualitative element in research design, there are many practical methodological difficulties to negotiate at data collection level. These include the familiarity of field assistants with different techniques, and issues of interpretation and comprehension by respondents. Rather than clear, general guidelines, addressing these requires a lot of flexibility and ingenuity, and willingness to accept certain trade-offs.

## Communication and interaction in collaborative research

Issues involved in doing interdisciplinary research in a large collaborative research project are discussed in most detail by Eguavoen in chapter 6. ZEF's GLOWA-Volta project in which her PhD research was embedded is a typical example of 'sustainability science', aiming to do interdisciplinary research on water management in the Volta basin and to develop a decision support system to help regional decision makers to improve water resources planning. The chapter describes her efforts to find a place for herself and her research on household water in this project. Apart from being a question of interpersonal communication and personal commitment, interdisciplinary collaboration is in Eguavoen's view strongly dependent on the way the project is organised and planned, that is, the internal boundary settings that enable and constrain that communication and commitment. For national boundaries, Kuzmits in chapter 2 observes that

> "[b]orders mark spheres of interest and the reach of sovereignty. Living with borders forms peoples' attitudes towards the neighbours beyond and towards their intrusions into the own social space. These intrusions may deliver wanted or needed features as well as potentially harmful effects. As a result border management is always led by a composition of security concerns and thrust for cooperation."

It doesn't take much imagination to translate this to development research. Despite all being trained as academic researchers, part of the same broader community and history, once boundaries have been created, as disciplines, or otherwise, boundary guarding and boundary crossing become complicated issues, notwithstanding an overall common interest in 'integration'.[8]

One organisational device in large projects that can easily be divisive in disciplinary terms is the so called 'work package', being the concrete unit in which the overall research is subdivided and conducted. There is a tendency, also known from other projects, to do such subdivision in a disciplinary fashion. One way to understand is that this reduces the transaction costs of 'integration', which is then made into a separate work package that usually has its largest time allocation towards the end of the project. A view of science that believes that problems can be cut up in their constituent part which can be put together again, the whole not being more than the sum of the parts, supports such an approach. Yet another factor is the often implicit 'hierarchies of significance' that Eguavoen mentions which define which discipline and research component is more equal than others. This raises rather fundamental questions about ontology and epistemology, subjects usually not explicitly addressed in the design of collaborative research. Such a 'disciplinary organisational design' is by no means necessary or unavoidable, and in 'integrative projects' it is explicitly not intended, also not in this project. However, it resonates with the dominance of (positivist and reductionist) disciplinary

science, and the individual preferences of many researchers, and seems difficult to avoid.

These larger issues play out at the mundane level of conducting field
research, and how this happens is the subject of Eguavoen's chapter. This is
also where some of the solutions to the problems of collaboration and integration lie. They lie at least partly at the level of creating conditions for con-
structive personal interaction, which can be induced by devoting time, human
and financial resources and some ingenuity to the design of organisational
arrangements for it. This requires rethinking of standard project design features both on the researcher and funder side. Technological devices like web-
sites and web-based data-bases may be important, but these digital artefacts
cannot replace, and do not automatically constitute, collaborative interaction.
Devoting energy to creating conducive organisational arrangements is all the
more important because also in the case discussed by Eguavoen, turnover of
staff and students is high.

## The political and ethical legitimacy of research

Uzbekistan is a country where research easily acquires dimensions of political
sensitivity, as is clear in the papers of Wall (chapter 7) and Veldwisch (chapter
8). This may be caused by the fact that field research is a very unusual thing
to do to begin with. In addition, research on rural development issues necessarily touches on state policy, which is not a neutral topic in an authoritarian
context. Rural development research has to operate in a context characterised
by secrecy and distrust, where discomfort and danger for respondents exist
because the secret police is monitoring the research of international projects
at least at a distance, if not closely, and by several other factors. For Kyrgyzstan, Wilkinson's analysis in chapter 3 vividly illustrates this – the topic of
research being security further enhances the point. Cross border activities in
the Amu Darya region as studied by Kuzmits in chapter 2 are politically sensitive in several respects, not in the least because drug trafficking out of Afghanistan is part of these activities, and basically inaccessible to field research.
Therefore, one level of discussion is that of political sensitivity of topic and
method, which makes it necessary for researchers to be very careful, invest a
lot of time in rapport building, and sometimes radically adapt method in favour of locally acceptable modes of conduct, and find ways to assess the
information and perceptions gathered from local respondents.[9]

Regarding the latter point, Wall identifies three types of subjectivity of respondents that influenced the information and perspectives they were willing to volunteer to the researcher. In the case of situational subjectivity a person's position's in society determines answers. Answers reflect a particular location and are 'situated knowledge'. Such information and perspectives should thus be contextualised to be understood properly, rather than being taken as a measurement of the diversity of individual experience and perception. Protectionist subjectivity is manifest when responses are driven by shielding oneself from danger, loss of face, or other risks. Reactive subjectivity lastly, refers to people changing their behaviour when they realise they are being studied. These problems exist in much, perhaps most, field research, but they take on strong forms in politically difficult environments, and raise the question what degree of 'strategic behaviour' of a field researcher is acceptable in this regard.

Nevertheless, even in such difficult environments learning the local language and immersing oneself to a considerable degree in everyday life of the society and communities studied, can go a long way in overcoming such limitations, as Wall's and Veldwisch's papers show clearly.[10] Wall and Veldwisch both conclude that participatory methods and observation are very important in such conditions.

As Veldwisch also notes, however, such circumstances and required adaptiveness may affect the validity of the research findings, and creative use of triangulation methods is required in response, reinforcing the point that methodology partly has to be made during the field research activity, and that this exercise itself provides certain types of insight, even when it also implies having to accept certain 'data gaps'.

Such circumstances raise the question how to position oneself as a researcher, and what political and ethical principles to adopt. For example, Wall states that the researcher in rural Uzbekistan is expected to behave in a host-guest framework, in which the ultimate control lies with the host. Being a male researcher with a male host, this created a gender gap in his research in the sense that accessibility to women and their perspectives became less than desirable for 'gender balanced' research. Ideal(istic) notions on normative and methodological principles do not provide much guidance in such situations. Such a problem may not be fully solvable at the level of the individual researcher, but it may be better addressed at the level of the project of which the individual researcher is part.

One of the issues involved in political and ethical positioning is that of self-censorship. In ZEF's Uzbekistan research project every publication is scrutinised by the project management for potential sensitivities, harm to the project and harm to local partners and respondents. This situation evidently creates serious dilemmas for social scientists investigating state governance and management, but also seemingly 'technical' topics like fertiliser and water use can be sensitive issues as they are associated with state-controlled agriculture. However, the concerns are real given the context in which the research is done, and the longer term engagement that is part of the broader research project design. How to handle a strategic discussion on the 'politics of research' in such difficult environments is not evident.

A very different aspect of legitimacy is referred to in Palmer's discussion in chapter 5 of the phenomenon that quantitative data and results are often perceived to be 'more convincing', that is carry greater legitimacy than qualitative findings. Palmer shows, however, that for the topic he researched, illegal logging and timber trade in East Kalimantan, 'hard' figures are extremely difficult, if not impossible, to come by, no matter how useful they would be, and that everyone is well-advised to be very careful in using figures on this issue that do exist. A similar point arises in Eguavoen's discussion in chapter 6 when she discusses the disciplining effect on data requirement that the development of a certain type of decision support model imposes: not all kinds of data fit into this, quantitative data fit better and are preferred, and greater legitimacy becomes/continues to be associated with it. This point about 'the force of figures' is related to the often implicit, sometimes explicit, hierarchy among disciplines, where those using quantitative methods are valued higher than those using qualitative methods. No matter how long discussed, and how thoroughly critiqued, the notion is very tenacious, and very much part of everyday perceptions of (inter)disciplinarity.

## Concluding remark

The elements of methodological boundary work described are not meant to be an exhaustive list or treatment, as already indicated. One function this collection is meant to have is to give O'Leary's 'budding researchers' encouragement not to despair when they encounter similar difficulties in their own field research. At a broader level we hope to contribute to discussion on method that goes beyond treatment of field research methodology as recipe and practical skill. Field research methodologies have to be done, philosophically, technically and socially, and doing them is (hard) work that involves the negotiating of a complex set of issues and circumstances.

## Notes

[1] See Malinowski (1967). Also see Barley (1983). I thank Irit Eguavoen for suggesting a reference to this literature. Other contributors to the volume are also thanked for their comments on this introductory chapter.

[2] See the concluding section of Wilkinson's paper (chapter 3) on the working of a 'sanitized vortex' in the way we speak in professional voice.

[3] It is the title of Klein's (1996) comprehensive discussion of issues related to interdisciplinarity.

[4] The social study of science and technology has generated the notions of boundary objects and boundary concepts (Gieryn, 1983; Star and Griesemer, 1989)

[5] Cf. discussion in ecological economics on the question of the (in)commensurability of values (Martinez-Alier et al., 1998, 2001), as relevant in the use of EIA (Environmental Impact Assessment) tools for instance (Espeland, 1998).

[6] Bailey (1996:xiii) writes " "Besides careful record keeping and analysis, field research incorporates luck, feelings, timing, whimsy, and art. I can't teach students how to deal with those things. Nor can I teach many of the characteristics that field researchers need – such as good social skills, ability to cope with ambiguity, and unlimited patience and flexibility. Basically, I believe that if you want to learn how to do field research, you have to *do* field research. Also see Laws (2003), Mikkelsen (2005) and Thomas and Mohan (2007) for how to be systematically flexible or flexibly systematic.

[7] Palmer (chapter 5) also touches on the issue of team management.

[8] Interestingly, all questions Kuzmits asks in his chapter about trans-border relations in the Amu Darya region can be translated to relevant questions about the relations among disciplines enrolled in a joint project. Such an exercise would be relevant if Eguavoen's recommendation to take boundary management work more seriously (fully in line with Cash as referred above) would be followed. Contributions on the designing of interdisciplinary re-

search like Moll and Zander (2006) and Pohl and Hirsch-Hadorn (2007) develop approaches addressing such questions.

[9] Two, of many, other examples of (potential) sensitivity related to ZEF PhD research are research on energy policy in PR China by a Taiwanese student, and a Malaysian PhD student trying to get a research permit for Borneo. As noted above, such (potential) sensitivities are perhaps more the rule than the exception in development research.

[10] Palmer in chapter 5 also touches on the issue of learning the local language.

# References

Bailey, Carol A. (1996) *A guide to field research.* Pine Forge Press, Thousand Oaks CA

Barley, Nigel (1983) *The innocent anthropologist: notes from a mud hut.* British Museum Publications, London

Becher, Tony (1989) *Academic tribes and territories: Intellectual enquiry and the cultures of disciplines.* Open University Press, Milton Keynes

Cash, David W., William C. Clark, Frank Alcock, Nancy M. Dickson, Noelle Eckley, David H. Guston, Jill Jäger, and Ronald B. Mitchell (2003) *Knowledge systems for sustainable development.* Proceedings of the National Academy of Sciences of the United States of America, published online May 30, 2003; URL: http://www.pnas.org/cgi/content/abstract/ 1231332100v1 (01/10/2006)

Espeland, Wendy Nelson (1998) *The struggle for water, politics, rationality, and identity in the American Southwest.* University of Chicago Press, Chicago

Gieryn, T. (1983) 'Boundary work in professional ideology of scientists.' *American Sociological Review* 48:781-95

Janesick, V. (1994) 'The dance of qualitative research design - metaphor, methodolatry and meaning.' In: N. K. Denzin and Y. S. Lincoln (eds.), *Handbook of qualitative research.* Sage, Thousand Oaks, CA, pp 209-219

Klein, Julie Thompson (1990) *Interdisciplinarity. History, theory, and practice.* Wayne State University Press, Detroit

Klein, Julie Thompson (1996) *Crossing boundarie. Knowledge, disciplinarities, and interdisciplinarities.* University Press of Virginia, Charlottesville and London

Laws, Sophie (2003) *Research for development. A practical guide.* Vistaar Publications, New Delhi

Malinowski, Bronislaw (1967) *A diary in the strict sense of the term.* Routledge and Kegan Paul, London

Martinez-Alierk, Joan, Giuseppe Munda and John O'Neill (1998) 'Weak comparability of values as a foundation for ecological economics.' *Ecological Economics* 26:277–286

Martinez-Alier, J., G. Munda and J. O'Neill (2001) 'Theories and methods in ecological economics: a tentative classification.' In: Cutler J. Cleveland, David I. Stern and Robert Costanza (eds.) *The economics of nature and the nature of economics.* Edward Elgar, Cheltenham, pp 34-56

Mikkelsen, Britha (2005) *Methods for development research and work. A new guide for practitioners.* (second edition) Sage, New Delhi

Moll, Peter and Ute Zander (2006) *Managing the interface. From knowledge to action in global change and sustainability science.* Oekom Verlag, Munich

Mollinga, Peter P. (forthcoming) *The rational organization of dissent. Interdisciplinarity in the study of natural resources management.* ZEF Working Paper

O'Leary, Zina (2004) *The essential guide to doing research.* Sage, London

Pohl, Christian and Gertrude Hirsch Hadorn (2007) *Principles for designing transdisciplinary research.* Oekom Verlag, Munich

Star, S.L. & Griesemer, J. R. (1989) 'Institutional ecology, 'translations' and boundary objects: Amateurs and professionals in Berkeley's Museum of Vertebrate Zoology, 1907-39.' *Social Studies of Science* 19:387-420

Stoll-Kleemann, Susanne and Christian Pohl (eds.) (2007) *Evaluation inter- und transdiziplinärer Forschung. Humankologie und Nachhaltigkeitsforschung auf dem Prüfstand.* Oekom Verlag, München

Thomas, Alan and Giles Mohan (eds.) (2007) *Research skills for policy and development: How to find out fast.* Sage, London (in association with The Open University)

Willis, Matthew (2005) *Shifting sands: conducting field research with ex-prisoners.* Conference paper. Australian Institute of Criminology Conference 'Safety, crime and justice: from data to policy'. Australian Government – Australian Institute of Criminology, Canberra. 8 pp. URL: http://www.aic.gov.au/conferences/2005-abs/willis.pdf (03/09/2007)

# 2

# Losing My Illusions

## Methodological dreams and reality in local governance research in the Amu Darya borderlands

## Bernd Kuzmits

## 1. Introduction

This contribution is intended as a type of 'workshop report' or 'thought piece'. It presents the hardships that a junior political scientist experienced in his field research on "Cross-border Interactions between Afghanistan, Tajikistan and Uzbekistan (across the river Amu Darya)". It portrays how this young fellow tries to combine his preferred political scientist's macro perspective with field research on the local ground. Further it delivers insight in how he tried to adapt himself and his skills to a delicate research area, in which all three countries provide various difficulties. Being this young researcher, I will try to introduce some field research challenges in a sort of systematic narration. As I do not consider them to be singular phenomena, I aim to tackle thereby three relevant dimensions of field research: the practical, the methodological and the ethical. Eventually, I intend to tell the story frankly. Consequently, in their pure naivety some parts might make more experienced researchers shiver. The less experienced though might get some useful lessons. As I conceive myself to be a representative of the latter ones, I will definitely usher into a learning process while writing this sketch.

In the following I first redraw the background and context of my research before introducing its content, methodological design and field research interest (section 2). The second section of this article is dedicated to the course of my field trips. Subsequently, I highlight, in section 3, some anecdotal experiences on timing, coping with bureaucratic impediments, expectation management, cultural sensibility and research in conflict zones that reveal aspects to bear in mind not only for field research in the borderland

areas of Afghanistan, Tajikistan and Uzbekistan. Section 4 gives some concluding remarks.


## 2. Background of research

The current study is part of the research project "Local Governance in the
Amu Darya Border Region" at the Centre for Development Research, University of Bonn (ZEF). The project which is funded by the Volkswagen
Foundation takes off at a historical starting point before the British Empire
and Tsarist Russia delimitated their spheres of influence along the Amu
Darya[1] at the end of the 19th century. The region was coherent, meaning for
the local population the river Amu Darya was a focal line rather than a borderline. Local people were linked by social and cultural commonalities, i.e.
among others kinship ties, language and belief. Also the power of political
entities did not end at the river banks. Some khanates on the southern bank
had to pay tributes to the Emirate of Bukhara. In the Pamir regions, the
khanates of Shugnan, Vakhan and Darwaz reached across the river. Eventually, the course of the river itself could not be clearly defined. Thus the river
did not mark the end of local peoples' mental maps. Much interaction was
going on across the river.

It is the core assumption of our project, that the ways how local people
settled disputes and organised processes to achieve commonly accepted decisions, how spoilers, who disregarded or violated decisions or rules were sanctioned (if they were), how the logic of local legitimacy works, in brief aspects
that make up the structural features of what we call nowadays local governance were similar on both sides of the river. This situation changed when the
Soviet Union started to fortify the border in the 1930s and literally closed it
later on. The river rendered a dividing line between different development
trajectories. The main objective of the research project is to trace the progress
of local governance structures in different state contexts or - as one might say
with a look on Afghanistan's recent history - in a non-state context. My part
of the project clings to the historical starting point that conceives the whole
region as a coherent area as my task is to observe cross-border interactions
once the gradual re-opening of the old borderline between new states started
after the demise of the Soviet Union. In doing so, I want to record the scope,
character and dynamics of today's relations and interactions across the long-
term closed Amu Darya river border. The analytical goal is to sketch the
ramifications for future trans-border relations.

## Content of research

Borders mark spheres of interest and the reach of sovereignty. Living with borders forms peoples' attitudes towards the neighbours beyond and towards their intrusions into the own social space. These intrusions may deliver wanted or needed features as well as potentially harmful effects. As a result border management is always led by a composition of security concerns and thrust for cooperation.

All three countries of concern are landlocked[2] far away from sea ports, dependent on trade and striving for access to international markets. It is an intersection of the political and economic regions of South and Central Asia with a border that cuts traditional trading routes. None of the countries has the capacities or the resources to generate a self-sufficient supply of essential goods or even sustainable economic growth. For this reason all these countries should have an interest to cooperate and maintain good neighbourly relations to warrant trade in order to initiate economic growth and to get access to markets. To date the aspect of cooperation gains weight in bilateral relations across this border and in border management.

On the other hand, the Amu Darya River runs through a conflict-prone region with weak states vulnerable to cross-border instigations of crises. Tajikistan's state and society are still recovering from a civil war (1992-1997) that took place while neighbouring Afghanistan was entrapped in seemingly endless war. The border between the two states still is a hot line for the smuggling of drugs and – decreasingly – of weapons. The process of Afghanistan's recovery has entered into a delicate situation that if worsening has the potential to severely affect neighbouring countries, e.g. by triggering off migration, by exporting instability or at least by hampering infrastructural or economic projects of regional cooperation.

The relations of the two post-Soviet countries, Tajikistan and Uzbekistan, are far from the former brotherhood of the people. In the wake of the civil war in Tajikistan, Uzbekistan had partly mined the border referring to insurgencies of the Islamic Movement of Uzbekistan (IMU). Relations between the two neighbours remain strained until these days. Mines planted by Uzbekistan along the border, which is only in parts delimitated, have not been cleared yet.

All these examples illustrate an ambiguity between needs to cooperate and fears of spill-over effects that characterizes the interrelations between the three countries. Obviously, this puts the aspect of control on top priority in terms of border management.

In brief, the core research question is:

*How do cross-border interactions relate to trans-border relations in the Amu Darya region between Afghanistan, Tajikistan, and Uzbekistan?*

And with an extension for comparative specification:

*Which differences can be detected between the three borderland areas considered on a bilateral basis (Afghan-Tajik, Afghan-Uzbek, Tajik-Uzbek borderlands)?*

At this stage, I have to introduce my concepts more closely. With cross-border interactions, I refer to any kind of bilateral activities across the border ranging from the movement of goods (trade in all its facets - legal/illegal, formal/informal), people (personal contacts, family ties, migration) and ideas (cultural exchange, attitude shaping information and ideologies).

My main set of questions concerning cross-border interactions looks like this:

- Who crosses the border and for what purpose (traders, commuters, labour and educational migrants, personal relations, political motivations)?

- Which goods and commodities are transferred across the border in which direction? Do they pass on to other destinations or do they mainly stay in the borderlands?

- How informal is border trade? Are some border areas more informal than others?

- How integrated are border economies with the economies of neighbouring states?

With trans-border relations I subsume the aspects of borderland governance, bilateral trans-border policies and local attitudes of the borderland population. Now, these terms need further exploration. When talking about *borderland governance* I refer to political measures (policies) and processes (politics) related to the border (*border management*) and the borderland. As mentioned above, border management ranges between the goal dimensions of security and facilitation of interaction. Whereas the security dimension encompasses policies that aim at the prevention of negative externalities (thereby putting up with constraints for interaction), the dimension of facilitation of interaction is on the contrary related to policies that are meant to allow positive externalities by fostering cooperation. Hence, there is a tension between the two goal dimensions of border management. The comparative interest of my study is to show the reasons for differences and perspectives for changes in border management. The aspect of borderland policies focuses on the status of the respective borderland regions within the state (state-periphery relation) and towards the neighbouring country (trans-national relation). This is done by assessing the state's influence in local politics, by screening for specific local borderland policies and by asking for *local borderland attitudes*. The latter component sheds light on the self-perception of the local population as being 'borderlanders' in a state context and 'frontier people' in an inter-state context. The scope of socio-spatial integration and distinction will be studied by applying concepts of socio-cultural perceptions of 'we' and 'the other'. Together with the evaluation of economic interests in cross-border activities and risk assessment, these data will be used to mirror the support for the specific orientations in borderland governance, border management and bilateral relations between security and cooperation.

In summary, the main questions related to these aspects are:

*For border management:*

- How porous is the border? How is it guarded?

- What are the legal prerequisites and bilateral agreements concerning border management?

- What are the state's priorities and capacities for border management? Have they changed and if so, why?

*For borderland policies:*

- What role does the referring borderland region play within the state?

- What is the state's policy towards this region? Are there specific political and/or economic programmes that distinguish this region from others?

- How integrated are border economies with the national economy?

*For local borderland attitudes:*

- Are people beyond the border perceived as being close or alien? What socio-cultural characteristics convey the conception of commonalities or distinction (ethnical, linguistic, attitudinal, spiritual)?

- Are there ties to people beyond the border? Of what kind are these ties?

- Do people favour or reject a change in the border regime? If they favour it, why and in what direction shall it be changed?

- If they reject, why? Do they fear migration or negative externalities?

- Do people expect more economic opportunities if the border regime will be liberalised?

One might rightfully object that my core research is much too broad. However, two methodological aspects connected to the design of our research project hindered me to pin it down more concretely. First, the subject of research is not a specific empirical problem or mechanism. At the beginning, there was neither the observation of a deficient material outcome nor one of a particular social setting. Both are classical drivers for political scientists to be treated as dependent variables for the generation of hypotheses on causal linkages with explaining independent variables. Rather, there was my vague role within the research project to cover the current processes of cross-border activities and trans-border influences on statehood.[3] For quite a long time, I was reluctant to abandon my political scientist's position and to quit the futile search for plausible causal relations.

Another fact aggravated this frustration. It is a distinctive feature of current processes that they keep on changing. For instance, bilateral relations of, say, Tajikistan to Afghanistan are as volatile as the security situation in the southern country. However, meanwhile cooperative measures take off not only on the local ground. Bridges are being built, consultative boards convene regularly and economic activities increase. However, it is too early to assess the impact for the local population in the borderlands. Here the second aspect hooks in: the multidimensionality and opaqueness of causal relations or the hen-and-egg-problem. Cross-border activities can provoke alignments of border management. On the other hand, border management may shape the scope and quality of movements across the border. But how can one trace back if a new border policy is actually a reaction to changes in cross-border activities? And which measures in border management did constrain if at all the general frequency of border-crossings. The reference that border crossings did happen in the region even before there was a perception of state borders does not lead any further.

So I had to refrain myself and learn my research mantra: Be modest in output ambitions! Observe and describe! This led to the following road map:

Within our research project I want to tell the story of this specific borderland region, a story of people living in borderlands where state structures are weak to barely existent and a story of the relation of these people to their state and to the neighbours. The reflection of my field research experience made me to content myself with the aim to pose the right questions. This may result in the sketching of preliminary scenarios and their conditions for being potential future processes. It is a modest but fair ambition in social science research. Roughly, the direction will be towards state building as a constraint for cooperation in areas where weak states meet.

### *Methodological design and field research interest*

But how do I tell this story? First of all, and here I stick to my roots, by applying the core method of political science: comparison. So I compared the interrelation between cross-border interactions and borderland governance on two strips of the Amu Darya border (the Uzbek-Afghan border, the Tajik-Afghan border[4]) and on the border between Uzbekistan and Tajikistan further north near the Tajik capital Dushanbe (see the maps and course of field research trips below). My conceptual framework for the scenarios will be taken out of typologies on borderland relations[5] and of theories on the conditions for cooperation.

At this point, it is helpful to recall how I initially wanted to tell my story, meaning to open my drawers, present my former design and then let it collide with the shock of field research.

**Table 2.1: Initial set of methods**

| Method | Objectives | Data sources |
|---|---|---|
| *Review of Literature and Documents* | to obtain information on the context factors for borderland governance and cross-border interactions | primary documents (agreements, laws), secondary and grey literature |
| *Actors and Network Mapping* | to earmark relevant actors, to visualize existing interrelationships and dependencies and to get insights in the logic and the stability of solidarity groups and local cross-border relations | interviews (questionnaires) with local people |
| *Open Interviews* | background information on the implementation of laws and agreements, on local governance and on the quality of cross-border relations | local decision-makers, domestic and foreign experts, |
| *Group Interviews* | to grasp self-perception as borderlanders, socio-spatial perceptions and constructions of 'we' and 'the other'; to detect key actors | 'borderlanders', local people |
| *Semi-Standardized Interviews* | to learn about assessments of borderland governance, to acquire information on types and scale of cross—border interactions and networks | local people, key informants and crucial actors, local and foreign experts |

As shown in table 2.1 actors and network mapping was at first part of the set of methods combined with the intention to study cross-border networks of crucial actors in the political economy of the borderlands. It was wiped out later by the understanding of the obvious. It takes a lot more time and a focus on two or three well pre-determined sites to implement these methods in a reasonable and efficient manner. Yet, I chose to cover a broader area and compare cross-border interactions, attitudes in borderland and border management. This deliberate decision brought out the political scientist in me, who takes the comparative position from a higher stance. For the sake of a more general picture which was also demanded by my project obligations I had to put up with more superficial impressions on the spot. Not only does it make a difference if one examines the Uzbek-Afghan or the Tajik-Afghan part of the border. Also along the Tajik-Afghan side, cross-border relations vary due to various reasons that can be traced back historically. I would have lost these important nuances if I had concentrated on just one specific area. And what should have been the justification for choosing one particular place and neglecting others? I fully acknowledge the outstanding importance of in-depth case studies, as I sometimes suffered from my forced superficiality. Yet, there is always a left-over for future projects. In this case, one could diffuse this study into a set of keen-eyed local observations.

Furthermore, the political economy of borderlands in this region is a sensitive issue as it consists to a good part not only of informal but of illicit activities. Drawing links between actors can turn out to be a hazardous endeavour. For this reason I was not actively interested in drug issues in the field although it is an important topic within my work. First, even if I had tried to trace drug chains across the border I wouldn't have received any significant information in a few weeks of field stay anyway. Second, I didn't even want to try for obvious security reasons. Equally needless to mention is that my remark on the open search for drugs in the field also applies to informal trade as a whole, as drugs are an informal commodity. Anyhow, with cautious observation it is possible to get a notion of the range of other less delicate informal borderland economies.

There were more caveats for other methods. Pursuing other objectives related to the study of politics as e.g. depicted in the table's row of open interviews (background information on the implementation of laws, local governance), would have been equally intense and time-consuming as an actors and network mapping. Further, given my time constraints at each spot, group interviews could only be organized with the help of an obliging key entry person. Considering the huge area to be covered only supported by occasional assistants, it was merely possible to note down typical samples of attitudes rather than representative positions.

As field research was constrained by other factors like bureaucracy, the organization of logistics and supportive structures and the intimidation through standardization (see below on cultural adaptations), the colourful bouquet of methods withered to little more than the basic skills of direct observation and informal conversation. This should not be confused with a "catch-what-you-can"-principle. It seems to be a classical process of a young fellow's research that it starts with methodological fireworks on paper and falls back on the seemingly boring ground of hands-on methodologies that are the bread-and-butter for every researcher, namely to observe and to describe. This works well, as long as it is led by a red thread. This was the basic set of questions listed above in my case. In the field it made me track along a certain routine. In doing so, as one of my first actions I always went to markets, compared prices and asked shop-keepers about their resources and position in the value chain. By the way, taxi drivers are a good source for ideas and information which naturally needs to be cross-checked and validated.

### Course of field trips

Field research was split into three trips of roughly three months each. As I travelled around a lot, I wanted to have breaks in between in order to reflect on results and modify my approach. Each trip was dedicated to one country mainly. However, to prepare subsequent field research trips for me and colleagues of the research project, I also crossed the borders several times. It would have been ridiculous anyway to write on cross-border interactions without undergoing this experience oneself. In spring 2006, I mainly stayed in Tajikistan, in autumn of the same year in Afghanistan and in winter 2007 in Uzbekistan. Maps 2.1-2.3 depict the trips in detail.

Together with the project manager I had already participated in two fact finding missions in the region. In terms of the organization of partners, indispensable for organizing documents and logistics, we were more successful in Afghanistan and Uzbekistan. As these structures were not settled yet in both countries and as I thought to have at least one promising entry person in Tajikistan, I started there.

The first two weeks of the first field trip (map 2.1) I spent in the Tajik capital Dushanbe taking expert interviews. I concentrated the following two weeks in south-west Khatlon around Sharituz before heading on across the border to the Uzbek city of Termez from where I made short excursions within the province of Surkhondaryo. Then I returned via Denau to Dushanbe from where I drove after a couple of days to Gorno-Badakhshan staying in Qalaykhum/Darvoz as well as in Khorog for a week. From Khorog I flew back to Dushanbe, starting point for a trip south to Afghanistan, where I stayed for exchange of experience with my colleague and preparation of my second field trip. On my way back, I stopped over for a week in Qumsangir on the Tajik side of the border from where I passed on to Kulyob, base for excursion to border villages in south-east Khatlon. Finally, after another ten days I went back to Dushanbe.

**Map 2.1: First field trip**

Although Afghanistan was the focus of the second trip (map 2.2), I took a flight to Tashkent as I had to arrange visa matters and prepare my third field trip. From the Uzbek capital I crossed Tajikistan via Khodjand (in the north) and Dushanbe down to the Afghan border. In Afghanistan, I stayed in the provinces of Kunduz, Tahrar and Balkh mainly, with a one-week trip to the capital Kabul for expert talks. From Mazar-i Sharif I drove to Termez and flew back to Tashkent.

## Map 2.2: Second field trip

## Map 2.3: Third field trip

Similarily my third field trip started (map 2.3) and ended not in the country of main interest, which was Uzbekistan. The borderland province of Surkhondaryo can be reached quicker from the Tajik capital Dushanbe. Through Sharituz I took an overland taxi to Termez, base for my research in Surkhondaryo with excursions to various sites. A ten-days trip brought me to the capital Tashkent.

# 3. Anecdotal experiences from the field

### *When this strange researcher came to town*

Before I travelled into the field I was well aware that my interest in border issues could turn out to be a little delicate and make people suspicious. But naturally, only in the field I learned to what extent it really was. The perception of shakiness among the local population varied considerably as did sensitivity for my mission. In general, Afghan people were much more responsive and less suspicious than interviewees in Tajikistan and Uzbekistan. Also within countries, responsiveness differed spatially. Although one should not generalize on this, it is at least telling that e.g. in Tajikistan I met more supportive people in remote Badakhshan, an area with a specific border history than in Khatlon, a region where state control is much more discernible.

For "ordinary people" of our own personal surroundings, i.e. not necessarily in touch with social science researchers, it is sometimes difficult to understand the motives and objectives of this species. I always realized this, when I tried to explain my mother what I was doing in these remote countries. This is even truer for people in the three countries of interest without a strong tradition of social science. They often encountered me with mistrust or at least deemed my deeds to be worthless.

It is essential to truly inform gatekeepers and interview partners about your background, but nobody urges you to burden them with something they can't understand and that would only raise undue suspicion. I decided to present myself as a scholar who writes a book about the history and the people of this borderland region, which essentially is the truth. Even then, the following response was symptomatic – at least for taxi drivers: "So you are kind of an artist. You do something that is not of use for many other people but you." I agreed with this true and pleasantly harmless description.

## A delicate topic

When I first arrived in the Tajik borderlands from Afghanistan, in the district capital of Kabodiyon, I had hardly stepped out of my taxi expecting a friend to pick me up, when a young policeman approached me and asked me for my documents. While trying to find the right way to hold my passport and searching for a hint to my nationality he was knowledgeable enough to instruct me on alleged rules for foreigners in the Tajik border region. According to him I was obliged to have a special permit to enter this area of national interest. These were obsolete rules used for a blunt attempt to charge some money. However, I was well equipped with supporting documents from the German embassy and able to avert this attack on my purse. Anyhow, this very first sign that border issues are still delicate woud be followed up by another one pretty soon.

Two days later, I accompanied the country manager of an international non-governmental organization to the opening ceremony of a water user association close to the border. Framed by toasts on international friendship, brotherhood and – when people were told that I was German – the solidarity of all Aryans[6], I was introduced to the crucial persons of that village who agreed to receive me the next day. However, when I arrived the same people were utterly reserved and not ready to talk without a formal permission of the district governor. I learned later that on the very day of the opening ceremony, not far away from the village three Afghans were seized while trying to illegally cross the border.

Two weeks later, I crossed the border to Uzbekistan at Gulbakhor, a frontier post in the border triangle with Afghanistan and Tajikistan. Everything went smoothly and I drove to Termez where I registered at a hotel to stay for a couple of days. A few hours later, two men came knocking on my door and identified themselves as officers from the immigration and registration office, called OVIR in the Russian acronym. They impressed me by telling me when and where I had crossed the border. Further, they claimed that I had to register on the very day of arrival if I planned to stay in Termez as supposedly rules are stricter for the Uzbek borderland region. Yet the officers still didn't know what I planned to do in the borderland region. So they invited me for an interview with the secret service to their office.[7] Several letters of support, the draft version of a memorandum of understanding with the director of Termez' State University and references to Uzbek history as part of our research interest seemed to soothe the officers' professional suspicion. Finally, the secret service officer tested my opinion on the so-called 'events of Andijan'.[8]

History was repeating itself during my third field trip, when I studied the Uzbek-Tajik borderland region. I drove from Dushanbe to a small town called Pakhtabad on the Tajik side of the border near Tursonzade. I hardly had stepped out of the taxi and seated myself in a canteen when secret service men in civilian dress came in and asked me about the purpose of my trip. They asserted that foreigners need special permits for the borderland area and requested me to leave what I did. But with my assistant I made a stopover at a village nearby where I talked to several people who idly killed time on this sunny Sunday afternoon. I then introduced myself to the village mayor (*hokim*) who politely urged me to leave by warning me that in weekly routine meetings he was supposed to inform the secret service about any incidents like foreigners in town. The quite bullying behaviour of the secret service indicated an increased nervousness in this region. This was clearly due to Uzbek-Tajik relations that were at an all-time low at that moment. A few weeks before tensed affairs, had culminated in a skirmish between border guards at a post nearby.

These anecdotes show that borderlands are a delicate area of high symbolic quality for statehood. Control capacity is concentrated here, and guards are not paid for being talkative and open-minded. Even if I had had a special permit by the referring government to do research on border issues, this would not have warranted the access to information. Below, I will show why I did not even try to obtain these permissions. As a result, I tried to get access directly locally via unofficial channels while avoiding contacts with district authorities in the field and staying undercover. As the example on the Tajik-Uzbek border has shown, this did not always work out.

### Coping with bureaucratic impediments

In the case mentioned above, after being rejected by the village leaders in the Tajik Kabodiyon district, I tried hard to organise the requested special permission. It took me a week to get an appointment with the district governor. In this meeting I was promoting my mission armed with any kind of supportive letters and referring to a bilateral German-Tajik governmental agreement on the mutual commitment to support research. In the end, the governor was ready to issue a permit – but only with the consent of the provincial government and under the provision that an official representative of the district administration would escort me. Apparently the governor was frightened to take a decision of this scale autonomously while his deputy was present. As it did not look like a promising way to wait ages for another audience in the provincial capital with unpredictable outcome, I decided to stop these efforts and chose informal channels to interviewees in a neighbouring district. This was the very moment when I lost my illusions on the implementation of text-book methodologies in the field and started to incorporate flexibility as a vital part of my personal expectation management. My assistant and several representatives of local and international NGOs were very helpful in doing so. Thus, in this case, I opted for a strategy of circumventing local officials.

Another bureaucratic impediment was piling up of travel documents, i.e. visa related matters. Actually, rarely I had a problem in obtaining a visa as I always held all the documents required. The problems came with registration and extension procedures and consisted of extra investments of time, nerves and money. Regulations are not always transparent and some civil servants are inventive in creating new ones. However, while queuing up in front of embassies and registration offices I not only caught much on the conditions for local people who try to travel to their neighbouring country. I also learned to respect in future some thumb rules:

-   *Mind handling times of applications:* It takes at least two to three weeks before you receive a reply to your application unless you want to pay a fortune.

-   *Arrange visa and registration through accredited organizations rather than with the help of private persons:* I did this mistake in Tajikistan once as I thought to save money that way. Better pay some more money if you want to keep your friends and save money on unofficial expenses. Running for documents like certifications by the police guard of the quarter you stay at, means harassment for your acquaintances and yourself; the more so if the guards are not in their office.

But don't get me wrong on this: visa procedures and annoying regulations are nothing specific Central Asian.


### On timing

There are several reasons for hard times in getting talkative interview partners. Political reasons can not be anticipated if they are grounded in sudden events. And the reaction to these sudden events can not always be gauged at once. Overthrows or terrorist attacks are such events. Reactions to the notorious caricatures of Mohammed detection, on appalling photos of German soldiers posing with skulls and bones or on the Pope's contemplation on the relation between Islam and violence can serve as concrete examples for my field research. Given the blueprint of the protests against the caricatures, public outrage following the latter two examples remained surprisingly weak. Other impeding political circumstances might be predictable but protract for such a long time that there is no alternative than take it or leave it, i.e. adaptation under permanent risk assessment. Pre-election and post-election tensions represent such situations.

Instead, holidays are situations that can be taken into account by planning field research. Admittedly, it is not always possible to include all eventualities into the timing horizon. However, one should be prepared with cultural knowledge to assess what can be done. It may happen that one can't avoid to do research during *Ramadan*. If this is the case it requires a specific intercultural adaptability in timing interviews. For instance, during this month it is not reasonable to plan meetings in the afternoon just before dusk as interview partners will not be able to concentrate anymore.

### *Expectation management*

As indicated above, people tend to have a better understanding for the direct practical use of natural compared to social research. Admittedly, it is often difficult for social scientists to maintain an immediate linkage of their research to real life. Being far from producing common laws for development or guides for implementation, social research can rather provide a thorough understanding of mechanisms of behaviour. Such an understanding is of mere indirect use for practitioners but nonetheless essential. However, in the field social researchers will be confronted with very concrete wishes and problems of the local population. For instance, in Tajik Farkhor, in a desperately poor area near Kulyob, I was once 'taken hostage' for two days by the representatives of a community development organization and nearly suffocated in hospitality. When these people presented me a parade of their problems, it became clear that they expected from me some solutions. Maybe they thought that I was able to do so being an individual from a rich country not representing an organization and not spoilt by politics. Out of pity it is tempting to cover up complexes about an alleged lack of impact by overestimating research opportunities.

The risk that researchers will give false hope to communities is not confined to conflict research. But the danger may be even greater in situations of widespread distress and few external means of support. This renders it crucial to clearly and consistently explain the purpose of the research to community members at all stages of the research process and to be honest on one's own capabilities. Unrealistic expectations can be avoided if researchers work with operational agencies to ensure that findings are closely tied to subsequent actions. In such cases, however, there needs to be extremely clear communication between researchers and agency. Poorly briefed researchers can inadvertently have a negative affect on community-NGO relations, which may have taken several years to develop.

### Cultural sense & sensibility

It might be basics for social anthropologists, but it is worth to be reiterated. As an intruder into local peoples' lives, it is the researcher who has to acknowledge routines, respect local customs and adapt to the local rhythm. If you are unsure about various habits, it's better to ask your assistant or to observe and adapt rather than act too actively. Field research also requires flexibility in interview techniques. In Central Asia many interview partners (although by far not all) won't appreciate direct speech or a resolute check off of questionnaires. It is more purposeful then to work with open questions, to take your time even if you are short of it and to show interest in lengthy narrations of daily affairs. Concerning the use of technical devices, I mostly had the feeling that recorders irritated people. But there is clearly no golden rule. One has to ask and be sensitive. Sometimes permanent note making can intimidate already. So, be prepared to work with mind minutes.

Ideally, assistants should be cultural advisors. Even if one knows the language and is familiar with the culture, a sensitive assistant, with whom one can cross-check perceptions, contributes to a safe and substantial field research. And if one doesn't know the language, one should at least learn some basic conversational phrases. Adequate clothing is not a question of taste only but essential, especially for women. These sounds like travel guide recommendations, but they are essential if you want that local people appreciate your intentions. And it is unbelievable how many foreign fellows you meet in the field who neglect these simple basics.

In Afghanistan, I was once mocked by one foreignmer as an "ethno-cultural creep", only because I wore the traditional *shalwor-ye kamiz* from time to time while she denied to wear a scarf. But while she was wondering about irritated Afghans my clothing made me feel more comfortable in some interview situations, yet by far not in all. In my meeting with the director of the energy supply company in Kunduz I felt awkward in my garments as the director wore a suit. Our supposed "change of outfits" really edged my self-confidence during the interview because I constantly thought that my interview partner might feel ridiculed by me. If possible, it is always advisable to be well informed about the descent and educational background of the interviewees in advance to prepare for such situations.

Functional groups have their own culture and sometimes their own sense of humour. Humour is a subtle topic of interactions per se. This counts even more in intercultural encounters and in conversations with security personnel. Once at the Uzbek-Tajik border I made small talk with Tajik guards while they were controlling my documents. We sat in their office having a nice conversation and enjoying an old Louis de Funès movie. I was curious about the reason for the huge amount of trucks that waited on the Uzbek side of the border. Not daring to ask directly, I tried to casually embed my curiosity into our chat as an innocent "by-the-way". Of course, I failed. The guard grinned and said that the Uzbeks just work badly. He added that inferring from my question one might think that I want to find out something specific. I was kidding with a play on words when replying: "Well, yes, indeed I am an investigator, although a scholarly one".[9] His grimace signalled that this was not a good joke and that I was lucky not to have hit another less indulgent colleague.

### Research in conflict zones

Suicide attacks are still single events in North Afghanistan and not yet a serial phenomenon. However, the security situation has deteriorated. Attacks are not only targeted towards government institutions and military patrols or facilities anymore but have expanded to include civilian objects. Personally, I would never go to the country's south or to Iraq as insecurity is not bearable anymore. In the Afghan part of our research area, it is also indispensable to carry out permanent risk assessment for which one has to be part of the 'information economy'. This means that one has to find some trustworthy local information sources and cross-check their output. This helps to assess the situation after sudden events (see above about timing).

Referring to experience from field research in Afghanistan, Jonathan Goodhand challenges the conventional academic argument that insecurity makes it impossible to secure valid data and that serious research has therefore to wait until the fighting stops. He argues that armed with an understanding of the patterns and dynamics of conflicts, researchers can make informed decisions about when, where and how to do research (Goodhand, 2004). Conflicts are often characterized by dynamic and mutating patterns of violence. These may be spatially, temporarily or seasonally determined. For example, fighting in Afghanistan tends to follow a seasonal pattern, with the spring and summer being the periods of greatest intensity. Compared to Afghanistan's southern and eastern provinces, the North and West are areas where security risks are rising but still assessable provided one is equipped with the required communication devices, stays clear of military patrols and hot spots, and keeps low profile. Naturally, these requirements already limit the intensity of field research. But keeping a low profile and 'minding one's own business' may become an essential survival strategy. One has to be aware of the information economy and be sensitive to the needs and fears of conflict-affected communities. Confidentiality should be a primary concern. Privacy and anonymity are to be respected during and after the research.

As described in the previous paragraphs, it seemed to be advisable to me not to condition interviews with time-efficiency and utility considerations. Furthermore, when choosing subjects for discussion, researchers must identify which are more sensitive than others and thus likely to endanger research subjects. In my case, direct questions on the subject of the opium economy and on informal cross-border networks were inadvisable. Some subjects may be taboo because they are too risky while others, though sensitive, may be addressed indirectly. Researchers have to be constantly aware that while they are present for only a short time, their questions and the discussions they provoke may reverberate for a long time afterwards.

Moreover, the ethical component of research weighs heavier in conflict zones. Research may have unexpected negative outcomes. Like any other form of intervention, research occurs within an intensely political environment and is unlikely to be viewed by local actors as neutral or altruistic. Just as aid agencies are increasingly revoked to 'do no harm' and develop an ethical consciousness, so conflict zone researchers similarly need to develop a robust ethical framework to ensure that they do not inadvertently 'do harm' and that they remain open to opportunities to 'do some good'. The process of conflict manipulates information by promoting or suppressing voices. Researchers are part of this information economy and should realize that research necessarily involves making political and ethical choices about which voices are heard and whose knowledge counts (Goodhand, 2004).

Goodhand enumerates in his recommendations components of 'do no harm' in conflict research. As they go well beyond research in hot spots, I find it suitable to present them here. There is no virulent conflict directly in the research area. But Tajikistan and the north of Afghanistan are post-conflict and more or less still fragile regions to which these recommendations can also be applied. Some of this advice is related to research projects that encompass a larger group of researchers, which does not apply to our research project. Yet they can also be applied for smaller groups or individual research with assistants. To put Goodhand's suggestions in a nutshell, negative impacts can be to a great extent minimized by a sensitive selection of researchers/assistants aware of ethical issues, by predicting likely ethical issues, and by a detailed assessment of the research's likely impact on a delicate local situation and vice versa. During the research, researchers need to

- blend in with their surroundings, keep a low profile and not attract unwelcome attention to the research subjects or themselves,

- constantly monitor the security situation and analyse risk, particularly by listening to local informants,

- obtain informed consent,

- honestly examine the power-relationship between researcher and research subjects

- explain clearly the objectives of the research,

- develop methodological flexibility and adapt methods appropriate to the security risk and need for confidentiality,

- appreciate the value of restraint: to know when it is time to stop

After the research it is important to build links to local partners and plan follow-up activities so the research is not purely an extractive exercise.

## 4. Concluding remarks

In this contribution I generally reflected some typical challenges in field research based on my own personal experience. As it is meant to be a workshop report I do not claim to produce solid textbook rules but rather disputable considerations.

Our research project combined three difficult countries to do research in with delicate topics to be studied in a sensitive area. Many of the challenges described above can be countered with a thorough preparation in practical terms that includes linkages to reliable partners, the organization of logistics and required permissions and documents. This involves indispensable investments in time and money. But given a lack of transparency and volatility concerning regulations some investments may be in vain. Additionally, the official march through the local institutions does not always pay off if one can't afford the time to wait. It can rather turn out to be obstructing. Yet one should always have the backing of strong local partners and advisors (universities and the like) and the support of the embassy.

In methodological terms I lost some initial illusions. Some methods and tools simply were too vulnerable to practical impediments and didn't stand the test of cultural adaptability. In this sense, research for a good part comes down to the basic skills of observation, informal conversation and description. If one is ready to adjust, this doesn't have to be a frustrating experience of shattered methodological dreams.

Cultural sensibility, transparency on intentions and honesty about competencies are essentials of the ethical dimension of field research. These elements are crucial parts of 'do-no-harm'-rules for researchers. These rules might enlist the obvious, which is however often neglected in practice and thus worth to be reiterated.

# Notes

[1] In the upstream area to the inflow of the river Vakhsh, the river is called Pyandsh. I will name the stream Amu Darya when referring to it at full length. If necessary in a local upstream focus the name is Pyandsh.

[2] ....with Uzbekistan being even double-landlocked, which means that all countries bordering to Uzbekistan don't have access to the open sea.

[3] This is not to complain as I myself contributed to this part of the project.

[4] For pragmatic reasons, I will limit myself to some sections of the Tajik-Afghan border to be further determined below.

[5] I will among others rely on the works of Anssi Paasi (e.g. 2006) and Oscar Martinez (1994).

[6] In the search for historic glue in the process of the nation-building, the Tajik government discovered the ancient Aryan culture that had its cradle in Central Asia. It is a completely unhistorical, initially irritating but intentionally friendly gesture towards Germans to refer to a common Aryan culture. Lectures about the Third Reich will not be understood.

[7] It has to be highlighted that from Soviet times until only a few years ago Termez with its military garrison was a city of national interest closed for foreigners. As the change of this situation and information on new requirements are intransparent, even the military attaché of the German embassy doubted in preparatory talks one and a half years before that it would be possible to enter the city without a special permit.

[8] It is difficult to depict these 'events' that happened on 13 May 2005 in the Uzbek city of Andijan (Ferghana valley) in a nutshell as there are various perspectives and independent investigations have been blocked. Roughly stated, there were seemingly three incidents: a jailbreak, a demonstration and the shootings. Imprisoned members of the Islamist group Akromiya were freed by armed backers. At the same time, there was a demonstration in the city mainly against restrictions on trade. On their escape the inmates and their backers mingled with the protestors. Uzbek Interior Ministry and National Security Service troops fired into the crowd. Estimates of casualties range from between the official number of 187 (most of them Islamist terrorists in the official Uzbek wording) and several thousands.

[9] I used the Russian word "issledovatel'", which has two meanings, researcher and investigator.

# References

Anssi Paasi (2006) *Boundary studies and the problem of contextuality*. Linea Terrarium, International Border Conference, El Paso, Ciudad Juarez, Las Cruces

Goodhand, Jonathan (2004) 'Research in conflict zones: ethics and accountability.' *Forced Migration Review* 8: 12-15

Martinez, Oscar (1994) 'The dynamics of border interaction, New Approaches to border analysis.' In: Clive H. Schofield (ed.) *World boundaries, global boundaries.* London, Routledge

# 3

# Positioning "Security" and Securing One's Position

## The researcher's role in investigating "security" in Kyrgyzstan

Claire Wilkinson[*]

## 1. A retrospective introduction

> "Life must be understood backwards; but it must be lived forwards."
> (Kierkegaard)

Kierkgaard's aphorism in many ways sums up the problem of conducting research involving fieldwork: one has to go and actually do it before one can start trying to make sense of whatever is the subject of the research. This paradox can seem especially troublesome when an interpretive methodology is being used, since the writing process itself is a central part of achieving a coherent understanding of the research topic. On the one hand, as I have experienced writing this paper, the researcher wishes to lead her reader on the same "journey of discovery" as she experienced in the field, hoping to show how insights were gained and conclusions made. For the reader, however, this is often a frustrating and confusing exercise, for simply being shown is not enough; additional explanation is required to allow even the most engaged reader to understand. Moreover, a reader instinctively wants to know where a piece of writing is going, and, equally importantly, how to get there.

This point was brought home to me reading the comments made by one of the reviewers of the first draft: "The current set-up of the paper seems to provide enough room to expand it a bit with a more systematic description of the research objectives, activities and outcomes." I bridled when I read it, underlined it, reread it and felt frustrated. Didn't the reviewer see that the whole point was that my research has ended up with objectives only in the very broadest and formal sense? That describing "research activities" brings me back into the dry, formal, capable style of writing so familiar from formal research reports that I wish to challenge in the name of authenticity (whatever that means)? Most worryingly, I don't know what my research outcomes are yet, other than more uncertainty and questions. Sure, I've got hunches and themes I want to write about, but not *outcomes*. Despite my frustration, it was clear the reviewer had a solid point: to make this text (more) accessible, more systematic explanation was required to help guide the reader in understanding it. In effect, what are the answers to the basic questions of where, what, who, and when in relation to this paper, and the research? The purpose of this introduction is to begin answering these questions, in conjunction with some general editing, clarifications and footnotes.

The very basic response to the "where?" question is Kyrgyzstan – the smallest of the five ex-Soviet Central Asian republics. More specifically, my fieldwork was carried out in the capital, Bishkek, for four months, followed by a further three months in the southern city of Osh after a break of a couple of months spent mainly in the UK. What? is a more difficult question. My original objective was to investigate ethnic identities and how these identities relate to perceptions of security. I was going to carry out mono-ethnic focus groups with Kyrgyz, Russians and Uzbeks to find out how they saw their identity and relations with other ethnic groups.[1] The events of March 2005, which culminated in the ousting of the then-President, Askar Akaev, after several months of protests sparked by the rigging of parliamentary elections, made the very possibility of conducting fieldwork seem less certain. I felt far less sure of my knowledge of Kyrgyzstan, which had been gained whilst a student there several years earlier, as I read dramatic accounts of events in aftermath of the so-called "Tulip Revolution" that included regular public protests, slightly less frequent assassinations and predictions of impending societal collapse.[2] I stopped talking in definite terms about my planned fieldwork, preferring a pragmatic "wait and see" approach. The next six months were spent following events in Kyrgyzstan via the internet, very much aware that I was getting a very particular and partial version of events that probably sounded far more dangerous than it actually was. Most of all, there was a growing sense of needing to reconsider one's perceptions of dominant dynamics in Kyrgyzstan. It seemed that nothing could be taken for granted anymore; everything should be looked at as openly as possible, questioning one's assumptions. This, as I shall discuss in section 2, set me firmly on the path towards an interpretive methodology.

Before I turn my attention to what actually happened to my research plans, there's still the "what" question to deal with. What did I actually do for my fieldwork, what data did I collect? To retreat into the anonymous passive voice, in keeping with "proper" academic style, a general answer would/should probably run something like this: Two periods of fieldwork were conducted consisting of four months in the Kyrgyz capital, Bishkek, (September 2005 – January 2006) and three months in the southern city of Osh (March – June 2006) with regular trips to Bishkek to observe public protests. In both locations a number of methods were used to locate and follow the dynamics of securitising moves and securitizations in the societal sector. In addition to the collection of Russian-language print media sources[3], a major source of data is interviews with representatives of ethnic (Russian, Uzbek, Uighur), professional (journalists, NGO sector), youth and sexual minority groups, as well as representatives of international organisations (UNDP, OSCE, IFES, Peace Corps). In Bishkek a total of 25 semi-structured interviews were conducted, and a further 13 were conducted in Osh. In addition a social survey using nine multi-part open questions was undertaken to ascertain local understandings of identity-related issues. The survey was administered by local research assistants and the final sample size was 544 (Bishkek n=291, Osh n=253). Responses were then coded and processed using SPSS. Observations of public protests (documented with photographs) have been used to ensure as inclusive an approach as possible to locating security narratives in Kyrgyzstan in conjunction with local Russian-language print media coverage. Secondary data sources used include speeches and statements made by Kyrgyz government officials and reports and surveys from international organisations, chiefly the locally-based Foundation For Tolerance International's Early Warning for Violence Prevention bulletins.[4]

All of the above description is accurate. The problem is that this doesn't tell even half the story. It doesn't tell you how I negotiated access to my interviewees, or how or why I decided to interview these people in particular. What did I document and why? What was the motivation for doing the survey when, like so many social scientists, I am sceptical of statistics at the best of times? (This was exactly why I chose to do it – to see how the results could be affected by contextual factors.) What language or languages did I work in? Did I use an interpreter? Why didn't I make an effort to learn Kyrgyz, which is, after all, the state language?

Answering such questions in detail, I believe, is vital for understanding my (and anybody else's) research. The language issue is an apt example: I conducted the vast majority of my interviews in Russian and, barring a few "lost-in-translation" issues,[5] it was unproblematic. There are several reasons, all specific to my research context that explain this. Firstly, although Kyrgyz is the state language, Russian has official status as a language of interethnic communication. Kyrgyzstan's history as part of the USSR means that Russian is still widely spoken either as a first or second language and despite efforts to linguistically Kyrgyzify politics and business, remains more widely used than Kyrgyz. This is especially true in the historically more Russified north and amongst elite groups, many of whom consider Russian their preferred language regardless of their ethnicity. In light of this, Russian is *de facto* a local language and in urban settings is widely used. Secondly, I already spoke Russian to a high level having taken my undergraduate degree in Russian and was comfortable using it to conduct taped interviews. These two factors meant that *for my fieldwork* Russian was the most appropriate language.[6] Indeed, trying to learn Kyrgyz would have closed off Russophones of all ethnicities, while Uzbek would also have risked aggravating many Kyrgyz, given that Uzbek-Kyrgyz relations are historically tenser than other interethnic relations.[7] I did consider working with interpreters if using Russian proved impolite or impossible, not least as while in Bishkek I was often told than no-one in Osh spoke any Russian at all, but it turned out the groups that I wished to talk with, and most other people, were happy to speak with me in Russian as the common language of communication.

As this seemingly simple example illustrates, to properly situate our research we have to at least partially step back into the disordered, confusing, illogical, serendipitous world of fieldwork experiences. Language was only one minor aspect of my fieldwork on a practical level, yet explaining the situation helps to provide as full a picture as possible, both of the country, but also of the research and the researcher. This is the subject of the rest of this article.

## 2. A methodological "confession" and the demise of a theoretical plan

> "As graduate students we are told that 'anthropology equals experience'; you are not an anthropologist until you have the experience of doing it. But when one returns from the field the opposite immediately applies: anthropology is not the experiences that have made you an initiate, but only the objective data you have brought back." (Rabinow, 1977 quoted in Whitehead and Conway, 1986: 2)

It often feels that we are supposed only to show the "product" of our research, not the "process", so I want to start with a confession: my research is the product of circumstance, of serendipity and coincidence, of contingency, of interpretations and being interpreted. I am not an anthropologist in any formal sense, other than by "accidentally" using methods that can broadly be defined as ethnographic. I did set out with a "Plan", a methodology, detailing which groups I was going to talk to, what methods I was going to use, and how my empirical fieldwork would relate to my chosen theoretical and disciplinary approach, namely Security Studies. For a number of reasons, as I shall explain, this "Plan" did not live long – something I felt guilty about at the time, and very relieved about now; as it turns out, Rabinow's observation is no longer axiomatic, even if that is not yet widely recognised, let alone accepted in the discipline of Security Studies and the wider fields of International Relations and Political Science.

Arriving in Bishkek, logistical issues rapidly caused me to reconsider what I would actually be able to get done; "hitting the ground running" was not going to be possible, not least as there were more pressing matters to attend to like finding a place to live. Institutionally, I did not have the resources, contacts or facilities to carry out focus groups. More generally, and more worryingly, it quickly became apparent to me that I needed some time to "tune in" to events and opinions and how they were being interpreted – and how I was interpreting them, on the basis of the information that had been available to me until my arrival (Russian- and English-language media sources with all associated problems of bias and selectivity). I was suddenly painfully aware of the need to question my culturally-subjective interpretations of interpretations, even if it meant coming up with the same answer at the end of the process.

This awareness, underlined by developments in my understanding of the limitations of my theoretical approach and how it results in a selective interpretation of events due to underlying Western norms (Wilkinson, 2007a), left me feeling very uncertain about how to proceed with fieldwork. There was a fundamental decision to be taken: to allow the theory take precedence despite recognising that it would "edit out" many of the processes and interlinkages in narratives of "security" in Bishkek, or to worry about the theory later and concentrate on building a more comprehensive – and therefore broader – picture of "security" in Kyrgyzstan and how people related it to their lives, identities and communities. The decision to use broadly ethnographic methods was largely intuitive; it felt like the only way to start "making sense" of everything I was aware of in circumstances of rapid socio-political change,

multiple and often competing public voices (not to mention the si-
lent/silenced ones), limited reliable information and the importance of informal politics and networks. It was also the most practical option. It also
made it possible to focus in on "locally attached meanings", key to understanding how processes actually work, rather than how one thinks they work.
Whilst it was the logical thing to do, it is not an approach generally advocated
by International Relations and related disciplines that have traditionally given
short shrift to ethnographic methods.

As with any decision, my change of fieldwork plan has had consequences, not least for presenting my research. If fieldwork requires an awareness of the double hermeneutic[8], then writing requires what Yanow has called
a triple hermeneutic, with the third interpretive moment occurring "during
deskwork while reading and rereading field notes and analyzing them, and
during text work, while crafting a narrative that presents both fieldwork and
analysis." Yanow further notes the existence of a fourth interpretive moment,
which does not belong to the researcher but to the reader or listener: how
you interpret what I'm saying (Yanow, 2006: 4). This is dependent on my
ability to reflexively draw on my ethnographic experiences to create an account of ethnographic comprehension, which is defined as "a coherent position of sympathy and hermeneutic engagement" (Clifford, 1986 quoted in
Bishop, 1992: 154-5). Traditionally, this has involved going back and editing
out the messiness of one's fieldwork, of tying up loose ends, of systematising
and showing the step-wise progress of one's research (which may not have
ever actually happened), of relabelling experiences to fit the expected criteria
of "validity", "rigour", "testability" and other "scientific" terms.

But is this actually the best approach? Broadly speaking, prior to fieldwork my plan was provided by my theoretical approach, which I was going to
go and apply to Kyrgyzstan. The Copenhagen School's approach to security
is founded in the concepts of securitisation, sectoral security and Regional
Security Complex Theory.[9] The central notion is that security is conceptualised as a "speech-act" (i.e. by saying security something is done) rather than
as something objective that is just there to be found; instead, security is dis-
cursively constructed by the person or group invoking "security" in the name
of an object, value or community, and the audience.[10] The attraction of this
theoretical framework is that the aim is not to simply apply the theories to a
given situation, but also to examine any problems that arise and attempt to
explain them (Buzan and Wæver, 2003: 49), creating a potentially reflexive
approach to analysis. However, theoretical potential does not always translate

into empirical practice; as one political scientist observed sorrowfully, reality has a nasty habit of interfering with theory.

Thus my fieldwork turned out to be more a case of applying Kyrgyzstan to Copenhagen School theory rather than the more conventional application of theory to case study. Inevitably, such an inversion led to the use of methods broadly known as "ethnographic" to create a "thick description" account of Kyrgyzstan and the events that took place between October 2005 and January 2006 and March to June 2006. In ethnographic terms, these two periods were not particularly extensive – and almost certainly would have been inadequate had I not already been familiar with Kyrgyzstan due to having previously lived in Bishkek for a year as a student at the Kyrgyz-Russian Slavic University. This gave me the added head-start of speaking sufficient Russian to be able to operate largely independently, as well as some contacts who already knew me personally[11] and who provided vital support in several respects.

Given the need to improvise a methodology in response to circumstance and the unexpected, this prior experience was invaluable. However, I realised this relatively late in my fieldwork, due to trying to be a "real" Political Scientist and consequently maintaining that ethnography was not what I was about. The blinkered nature of such a stance has not been missed by all political scientists, as Bayard de Volo and Schatz note: "The irony is that although political scientists, as students of power and politics, are well positioned to consider these links, the discipline tends rather to ignore them" (Bayard de Volo and Schatz, 2004: 268). In the field, however, it made more sense to ignore the discipline and concentrate on "being there", observing, experiencing, listening, participating and, always, questioning, regardless of how relevant or not it might seem at the time. By extension, as I have discovered, all of these processes continue once one has left the field during the "deskwork" and "textwork" of processing data and creating one's analysis: reviewing events, perceptions, reactions, rereading interviews and printed sources, re-examining photographs. The difference is that one is able now to see the "bigger picture" of one's research and begin to explain what was done and why.

## 3. The research practice: what is security, anyway?

"What is security... Security is when one feels confident in oneself and protected. At the moment, I think, no-one in Kyrgyzstan feels secure, because the political situation is unstable."[12]

"For me security means when nobody intrudes into my personal life, when nobody hurts me, when my rights and beliefs are respected. ... Security is when you just know that your day will be calm, free of stress or negative experiences, ... security is when nothing threatens you."[13]

"[Security is] a certain activity that doesn't cause harm to the state."[14]

Of all of the 25 interviews I conducted in Bishkek, only members of Kel-Kel, a youth organisation that was a high-profile actor in protests leading up to the "Tulip Revolution" immediately moved for a definition related to the state rather than considering a number of levels. Most often I was left wondering when talking about security – *besopasnost* in Russian, the language I worked in – if it would be more accurately understood as "security" or "safety". Once linked to notions of identity, both are equally relevant and often understood as two parts of the whole: safety deals with the immediate environment and threats to one's physical wellbeing, whereas security adds the "tomorrow" dimension, the answer to the "do we have a future?" question.

In theory, this linguistic hair splitting shouldn't pose a problem: it is simply a matter of returning to the Copenhagen School's criteria for when a securitising move has occurred: firstly, the issue in question must be presented as an existential threat and justification is being sought to handle the matter using extraordinary means, breaking normal political rules (Buzan, Wæver and de Wilde, 1998: 24). In more rhetorical terms, the logic is "If we do not tackle this problem, everything else will be irrelevant (because we will not be here or will not be free to deal with it in our own way)" (ibid.). This rhetoric is then voiced by someone speaking on behalf of the collective. Identifying this "we" should be quite straightforward: it is a societal (rather than political)[15] community identity with which people self-identify and which may be considered to be relatively stable or "socially sedimented" (Buzan and Wæver, 1997: 243). But people do not define themselves in isolation from events but more *in relation to* events even in stable environments; people use or refer to the most relevant identity or identities they have in a given situation. Yet again, I was left unhappy to the theory's objectivist conceptualisation of identity as I experienced how I was constructed and constructed myself in relation to events, interactions and exchanges, and tried to interpret other people's highly contextual, multilayered identities.

A primary example of this was the series of protests sparked by the killing of Tynychbek Akmatbaev, a parliamentary deputy, during a visit to a prison colony on October 20, 2005. Within 48 hours of Akmatbaev's death, the deceased's brother, the known criminal authority Ryspek Akmatbaev, had brought his supporters to Bishkek and set up camp opposite the parliament, calling for the resignation of Prime Minister Feliks Kulov, whom they held responsible for Tynychbek's death, alleging that he had ordered the killing to be carried out via his connections to the Chechen mafia.[16] This protest continued in Bishkek until October 25, with related public protests and demands for Kulov's resignation being held in Osh on October 24, in Jalalabad on the 25th and in Karakol on October 26. At the same time, Kulov's supporters took to the main square in Bishkek on October 25 in a counter protest to demand that the President, Kurmanbek Bakiev, support his prime minister. Akmatbaev's supporters dispersed on October 25, after President Bakiev controversially met with a delegation including Ryspek Akmatbaev to discuss investigating his brother's death. By October 28 the issue had taken on broader significance, with a rally being held in Bishkek and 35 towns around the Republic under the slogan "Peaceful Citizens for Kyrgyzstan Without Organised Crime". Thus in an eight-day period there had been a total of 45 related public protests with three securitising moves. Firstly, Akmatbaev's attempt to portray Kulov as a threat, then Kulov's supporters' effort to cast Kulov as being in danger from criminals and the inactivity of the President, and, finally, the wider NGO community's attempt to portray organised crime (and, by implication, Ryspek Akmatbaev) as a threat to Kyrgyzstan, not least due to Bakiev's controversial meeting with the known criminal authority. In addition, in the same period there were also a further four public protests about unrelated matters.[17] In virtually all these cases, issues were presented by the protesters as requiring immediate action and as a danger to the future of the protesting group, if not society more widely, thus arguably fulfilling the "existentialist" criterion of the Copenhagen School.

The next question, therefore, is whether measures outside the realm of "normal" formal politics are being advocated to resolve the matter. By western standards, the answer is yes. People are operating outside formal sociopolitical mechanisms in favour of direct action, calling for solutions not sanctioned by legislation or formal politics – as was the case with demands for the immediate dismissal of the Prime Minister or for the immediate allocation of land regardless of ownership[18]). In doing so, they move matters beyond the bounds of "normal" politics and into "security". As for the required group identity component, the *we-feeling* necessary for an issue to be placed in the societal security sector, then the protest in effect constructed a group identity by virtue of participation, even if it is only a temporary phenomenon.

It became more and more apparent as I followed the development of the various protests, noting contradictions in how they were responded to (Bakiev's meeting on October 25 with a delegation led by Ryspek Akmatbaev springs to mind as a prime example of an "unusual" response), I was left feeling that the Copenhagen School's analytical tools weren't quite as sensitive as I had hoped: there was no room for discussion of what constituted "normal" politics and who defines it – a fraught question in Kyrgyzstan even before March 2005 – and, even more frustratingly, no space to consider the questions "how" and "why" events developed in a particular way or people participated a particular protest or not and how it related to their lives and communities. Most importantly, and most worryingly, securitisation theory risked obscuring the interconnections between different communities, identities, and perceptions both within Kyrgyzstan and internationally. The importance of this "interconnectedness" was not lost on some of my interviewees, some of whom talked explicitly about it: "... I already want to emphasise again the extent to which everything has become interconnected. Waste uranium, or radioactivity, or air pollution, or something else, they don't look at ethnic or religious identity, they'll get everyone in succession."[19] In this respect, it often felt like everything or nothing was "security".

By this time my fieldwork had taken on a distinctly "ground-up" flavour with a view to trying to move from operationalising Copenhagen School theory towards critically interrogating or "problematising" it. This inevitably became a more self-consciously reflexive process (and still is) and also a less defined one. I wanted to consider identities that did not have the power to mobilise people – in securitisation speak, to see who couldn't "speak" security and why. My focus on ethnic identity became one of several: youth groups were added, as were journalists, international organisations, local NGOs and sexual minorities. Situating my interviewees remained important to understand their views; whilst they might speak primarily in a professional capacity, their personal interests, social status, age and other personal all influence what they say and how they say it. Furthermore, their answers needed to be seen in context, personally and societally. For example, media coverage about the "criminalisation" of Kyrgyzstan increased noticeably after the October 28 protest "Peaceful Citizens for Kyrgyzstan Without Organised Crime", which arguably heightened public perceptions of the influence organised crime had. Similarly, personal experience will inevitably affect people's responses, as illustrated by the following response to my question about what security is.

Despite the fact that the speaker was taking part in a group interview as a member of a youth political organisation, he spoke as much as a journalist – his profession – as an activist:

> "I don't have a clue what security is... Security isn't even a topic here at the moment, I'll just say one thing, everyone, probably, knows [...] they openly made threats by telephone, told me openly that if I didn't leave Osh they'd get me. I covertly took an interview from them, border guards came in, they weren't even scared to openly beat me badly. It was in Osh not long ago, around about the 6th or the 7th of December. So, what sort of talk about security can there be? At the moment on that count, I don't know."[20]

In this instance, in relation to "security", his formal situational identity as a representative of Kel-Kel being interviewed was temporarily overshadowed by his identity as a journalist who had recently been attacked. This shift was tacitly recognised by another interviewee as the focus was brought back to Kel-Kel: "I... I sometimes don't think that such simple questions will turn out to be so complicated. I'd like to note that Kel-Kel is a safe/secure organisation [i.e. does not pose a threat]."

Furthermore, whilst talking to people and conducting interviews, it became increasingly apparent that centring local knowledge and using it to consciously decentre normative assumptions (both my own and theoretical) was key to capturing as much of the local context as possible. In many cases this involved me deliberately asking questions that must have seemed at best naïve and at worst idiotic. It became apparent though that it was often an effective way of building up my understanding of the situation, often by making me rethink my opinion, and had the significant advantage of helping my respondents make explicit the interconnections they saw between themes and groups. Vladimir Tyupin's answer to my question about the importance of sexual orientation in one's identity showed the range of references involved:

> CW: "Every person has their own identity. There are many aspects of it. But in my opinion, given my personal experience, my sexual orientation is more important than, say, that I am English. It plays a more important role. How do you think sexual orientation influences the formation of personality here? Is it like everywhere, or there are some differences?"

> VT: "I think it's like everywhere. These people face the same problems as in other countries. And of course, first of all they want to organise their private life according to their sexual orientation. Nationality comes second... They try to associate with the people like they are, not nationality- but personality-wise. But when the circle of contacts is wide, the division begins: this is a Kyrgyz circle, and this is an Uzbek one. Europeans, Russians enter all cir-

cles, they are more or less neutral, but those try to keep themselves to themselves. Everyone has their own traditions, certain groups consider themselves more elite so to speak. Just like Baltic people – they don't associate with Russians, this circle is below them. The same happens here. But mostly the division is social. Wealthy people form one circle. Common people and hangers out not earning good money will form another circle – irrespective of ethnicity."[21]

The focus moved rapidly from sexual orientation and an international commonality of experience to what identities people use in different situations and factors influencing these choices. Furthermore, Vladimir's answer contained a good deal of analysis: he notes the importance of ethnic divisions and cultural background in broadly post-Soviet terms before focusing on Kyrgyz and picking out what he feels is a primary marker and organiser of society in Kyrgyzstan – or at least, in Bishkek.

This process is, inevitably, highly subjective. After all, it is my reading of someone else's interpretation – a classic example of Gidden's double hermeneutic and one that highlights how in the case of fieldwork, our "material" is intersubjectively created and embedded in multiple meta-narratives. However, the Copenhagen School stops in a position Eriksson describes as "observe how others advocate!", ignoring, if not denying, the influence of the analyst or researcher. Whilst this might be tenable theoretically, empirically it is extremely limiting. In contrast, Eriksson argues that "the role of the analyst cannot be to observe threats, but to determine how, by whom, under what circumstances, and with what consequences some issues are classed as existential threats but not others" (Eriksson, 1999a: 314-315). Even this statement, though a welcome extension of the Copenhagen School's objective constructivism, denies the active role the researcher plays in the construction of the analysis: Who is the Researcher, personally and professionally? What impact has she had on her research? After all, how an issue is reported to others will affect their perceptions and, by extension, their responses. Explicitly including the researcher is therefore vital to allow people to evaluate his or her claims fully by providing a strongly reflexive account of the research: not only is the pretence of "objectivity" rejected, but the researcher – me, in this case – seeks to situate both the research and herself within wider sociocultural, political and economic contexts (Presser, 2005: 2068) both on the level of the field and the broader culturo-spatial scales she operates in.

## 4. From speaking to negotiating "security": including the researcher

> "Where are **you**, dear Author, in this research project? In reading documents and in interviewing topic-relevant actors, you are – we assume – acting out of your role as researcher. But in field research that is more participatory than just observational, researchers often adopt a situation-specific role in addition to their researcher-role, acting in keeping with the demands of that role when necessary." (Yanow, 2006: 20-21)

The notion of the fieldworker performing a role is not new, and in many ways it is an accurate reflection of how many of us operate, consciously considering our role(s) in the field and less consciously even when at home "off-duty". We often become more aware of the importance of how we are perceived in an unfamiliar setting, and use "props" to "signal" our role, much as an actor would. For example, I chose to wear formal suits much of the time in Bishkek, for a time grew my hair slightly longer, strove to speak formal Russian, had business cards printed as a status enhancer (anyone who is anyone has a business card) and generally tried to interact with people in my formal role as a researcher.

This performance of being a Researcher was very much a tactical choice based on previous experiences in Kyrgyzstan as an androgynous-looking female who is 180cm tall and solidly built, has short cropped bleached hair and has a tendency to wear jeans, loose shirts (never blouses – they're impractical and never fit) and work boots for all but the most formal occasion. Some female researchers have commented on using their femininity to their advantage in the field with male informants, acting "more female" than they feel they do otherwise.[22] Firstly, due to my appearance and its distance from local ideals of femininity and womanhood, I am doubtful that trying to act more "feminine" on a personal level (such as being coquettish or trying to be a "damsel in distress" to allow a male respondent to take control) would have had much effect for gaining access and it would certainly have increased my sense of personal discomfort. At the same time, it could be argued that I did act less stereotypically "masculine" way by putting myself in a subordinate position to my interviewee (similar to a teacher-pupil relationship) and thus being less assertive or forthright. I would argue, however, that this was done primarily within my status as a Researcher, not as a woman.[23] On the rare occasions that I noticed an effort to engage me on a directly personal and potentially (hetero) sexual level, I was quick to move the conversation back to more comfortable ground, either by making myself "unavailable" (phantom boyfriend syndrome), less stereotypically desirable (I'm too independent, too opinionated, I don't want children, my career/education is the most important thing for me, I'm divorced), or simply pressing on with whatever I wanted to talk about.

At the same time, I was very aware that my status as a young, unmarried, obviously western, female, though often frustrating, could also work to my advantage. This was particularly the case with personal contacts, where I was classed in effect as an honorary daughter or junior member of the extended family network to be helped and assisted. Nowhere was this truer than my relationships with several people I had known whilst at the Kyrgyz-Russian Slavic University (KRSU) as a student: on the one hand they were a great source of friendship and assistance, on the other I was aware that I had a role to play as a student and native English speaker who could be wheeled into English classes on demand. This was an archetypal situation-specific role, and one I was happy to fulfil, at least for the first month or so, as it provided me with a "way in" to my fieldwork at a time when I felt very out of my depth and unsure what I "should" be doing.

As I continued, however, I began to reconceptualise my role(s). Rather than trying to actively immerse myself in Kyrgyzstan as much as possible – the stereotypical idea of "going native" – I took a more "outsider" stance, which is personally far more comfortable, partly for reasons I will discuss below. This is not to say I was a complete outsider; obviously I associated with or was seen to be associated with various groups: expats, the "Europeans" (Slavic minorities), Russophones, educated professionals, staff and students of KRSU. Yet I still felt consciously more outsider than insider, even though it seems in most cases people perceived me on their terms, rather than on mine, so in terms of potential sources of bias my nationality, unusual appearance (by local norms), status as an unmarried woman (especially in Osh) and sometimes my lack of Kyrgyz were far more relevant for the people I interacted with. Even the fact that people would often read me as male did not carry the same implications as it would in a western setting,[24] due to the fact I was so obviously a foreigner in every sense of the word. Indeed, I was far more aware of not conforming to gender norms than others were. The extremity of my self-consciousness and the need to decentre oneself in the field was made clear in Osh: people often asked if I was an *americanets* (male American), and I always corrected them, saying I was an *anglichanka* (Englishwoman). Much of the time, the response would then be, "ah, vy anglichanin!" ("oh, you're an Englishman"). This became a source of concern and some anxiety to me over time, until I mentioned it to an extremely feminine volunteer worker one evening, only for her to reply that the same thing often happened to her. As I then realised, the issue was largely linguistic: in contrast to Russian, Kyrgyz does not have grammatical gender, and in contrast to Bishkek, people's knowledge of Russian is often more limited as Kyrgyz and Uzbek are more commonly spoken.

More generally, my perceptions and interpretations were affected by a different set of largely hidden biases: those of a gay woman who is used to being implicitly, if not always explicitly, "out", with all attending consequences, positive and negative. On a purely practical level, as Walter Williams noted, "I have found that my gayness is much less of a problem than the common obstacles facing most fieldworkers" (Williams, 1996: 70). Beyond everyday practicalities, however, my sexuality and my fear of being identified as gay was a large part of my sense of needing to maintain an outsider position, both for safety and in order to keep a sense of self and be able to switch off from performing situation-specific roles actively or passively. Ironically I was far more conscious of my visibility than local lesbians, seeing as in local terms I could be read either as lesbian or just as a western woman, as a member of Labrys made clear at a gathering. I was initially taken aback when she asked if I was actually gay, until she explained: "well, all Western women look like you, so how do we know?" I suspect I found this more amusing than many straight women would, given how often "lesbian" is used as a shorthand for "unfeminine" and masculine in the heteronormative world.

My being gay also undoubtedly influenced my decision to try and get in contact with both LGBT organisations, with my Researcher role providing a "safe" identity from which to negotiate initial contact, especially with Labrys, a youth group for lesbians, bisexuals and female-to-male trans people. I would suggest that their initial agreement to be interviewed hinged on me being a westerner and female, and therefore, in all probability, gay-friendly. The dynamic changed on meeting in person when they correctly read me as lesbian. Whilst all relationships change once people have met in person, the change in this case was to a more personal level due to the perceived shared experience of being gay and a sense of not having to explain oneself or answer well-meant but naïve questions about sexuality, for example.[25] This common identity helped make me, in some ways, an insider, both in relation to Labrys and Bishkek more generally, since I no longer felt so mentally and emotionally isolated: my fieldworker and home personalities could sometimes meet up comfortably once more.

With the exception of interviews with Oazis and Labrys, where I used my own gay identity as a common reference point, I presented myself as a doctoral student from a UK university and former student of KRSU. The former provided a certain status, whilst the latter provided a kind of credibility and source of trust, as it implied that I knew something about Kyrgyzstan and its history, and, perhaps more importantly, had a broader interest in the country than just my research. This active projection of my Researcher role extended to my "off-duty" persona in the field. Questions about my marital status, lack of husband/boyfriend and children could all be shrugged off to a greater or lesser extent by referring to my desire to complete my education first, and the need to stop travelling in order to have a family. At the same time I learnt that sometimes it was easier to give an understandable answer than try to explain what is to some extent unexplainable in local terms: particularly in Osh, saying I was divorced provoked no questioning, in contrast to trying to explain that 26 is still considered young to be getting married in "my" culture. Furthermore, in conjunction with my "Westernness", my Researcher role allowed me to bridge the gender gap, gaining a sort of "honorary male" status that mitigated local gender stereotypes about how and what a woman should be. I do not know if being viewed as a divorcee affected perceptions of me since I did not use this tactic with any of my informants, only in more everyday encounters to curtail the need for lengthy explanations or cut off a battery of personal questions, albeit sometimes unsuccessfully.

In many ways, these tacit negotiations of who I was (in a particular situation) and consequently how I should be treated was also beneficial to my informants as it absolved them of much of the need to heed local social conventions about hospitality, which are extremely powerful in Central Asia. Thus if I had arranged a formal interview, it could be completed with minimal ceremony and forgotten about, whilst when I visited KRSU it was acceptable for me to be treated still as a guest, but one who did not require an active and formal show of respect and hospitality. Where matters became more problematical was presenting my subject. Saying openly that one is studying security is a quick way to get bogged down in the very stereotypes one is seeking to avoid and also put people on their guard. Therefore I tended to present the issue in a number of ways, usually mentioning the words "society", "perceptions of security", "relations with the state", "identity" and "communities". On the one hand I feel this approach was warranted in light of the value-laden nature of words like "security", on the other I was aware of the danger of ending up speaking at cross-purposes and being misinterpreted. The matter was made doubly complicated by the dual meaning of the Russian word *besopasnost* as either "security" or "safety" in English, and it often seemed to me that people were talking primarily about "safety" in the sense of their immediate physical wellbeing. Therefore as a check, I chose to introduce a seemingly simple direct question: what is security for you? On its own this question would have been wholly inadequate, but within the wider context it proved to be very important in picking up nuances, contradictions and ensuring I did not leap to conclusions on the basis of limited information. In addition, from a theoretical perspective, it further highlighted the need to understand what we – and others – mean when we use certain words, since no word is value-neutral and our usage informed by a myriad of socio-cultural factors that require explicit interrogation by the fieldworker.

At the same time, my awareness of being an outsider based on my personal experience arguably made me more aware of gaps and silences in who gets to "speak" security in the public domain and in whose name. I was particularly interested in why some identities that people tend to feel are very fundamental to their sense of self – gender in the case of the social survey I conducted, sexuality in my case – proved incapable of generating sufficient cohesion to meet the Copenhagen School's criteria of a "we-feeling". In this respect I was able to use my awareness of how being gay affects how I see things, or a "gay sensibility" (Aldrich, 1992:27-28 quoted in Wafer, 1996: 261) to inform my research, or, more accurately, to add a different angle.[26] This is not to say that other people would not have been aware of such "silences", nor that there are not many more "silent/silenced voices" that I did not seek to include. At the same time, to not reveal the role my personality played in shaping my fieldwork in every respect vastly reduces the "I-witnessing" potential that is so central, indeed vital, to ethnographic methods. This is because I negotiated personal relationships and keeping a "safe" distance and selected which accessible identities I wished to include in my study. These processes were all informed by how I perceive the world around me with my own biases and sensitivities, and all of these factors are reflected in the research and its results.

## 5. Concluding thoughts: why positionality and reflexivity matter outside the field

"How, one asks constantly, could such interesting people doing such interesting things produce such dull books? What did they have to do to themselves?" (Pratt, 1986: 33 quoted in Doty, 2004: 378)

Many of the issues I have sought to raise in this paper are no doubt familiar to anyone who has conducted fieldwork. Yet, paradoxically, many of them get written out or relegated to a single sentence or footnote in the completed thesis or final report. This happens for numerous reasons: respectability, concerns about how one or one's research will be perceived (egocentric navel-gazing, for example, to pick but two dismissals), maybe even a feeling that revealing the "messy", personal side would reduce authorial authority. It is difficult to maintain the position of being an objective "expert" and dispassionate consummate professional when one admits to having personal biases and having chosen to include or exclude something or someone for personal reasons rather than "respectable" reasons such as logistics or not meeting some criteria. The result, as Doty describes with painful accuracy, is that

> "Our ideas, curiosities, intellectual wanderings, and ethical concerns are twisted and contorted to fit our professional voices and all the while the soul of our writing becomes eviscerated, our passions sucked into a sanitized vortex that squeezes the life out of the things we write about" (Doty, 2004: 380).

Both as social scientists and as human beings, we have a responsibility to "tell it as it happened", rather than how we would have liked it to be or a neatly edited selective account. The world around us is messy, interconnected and often chaotic. Simultaneously there is also order, patterns and systems. The challenge is to coherently integrate these two facets of the social world in our research, rather than seeing them as a dichotomous pairing: research being about the "mess", writing about order. Instead, we should be interrogating our interpretations of what we have been told, challenging our disciplinary and personal assumptions to create a reflexively analytical and multilayered narrative.

The researcher as a person is key to this process. For, as Wax argues, "in the field, one's basic humanity is emphasized, and such essential traits as age, gender, temperament, and ethnicity become, if anything, magnified in the process of developing interactions with strangers" (Wax, 1986: 130). This human aspect of research and its effects and implications should not be simply swept under the carpet as a messy inconvenience: it is what makes our research live, interesting, engaging, and, most importantly, credible.

# Notes

* This is a revised version of a paper originally presented at the conference 'Central Asia and the Caucasus: Explorations from the Field' at the Middle East, Central Asia and Caucasus Institute (MECAS), University of St. Andrew's, Scotland, November 10-11, 2006. Thanks to both reviewers and Dvora Yanow for their helpful comments.

1 One of the most often-quoted statistics about Kyrgyzstan is that more than 80 ethnicities reside in the Republic. As of 2004, Kyrgyz make up approximately 67% of a total population of 5,037,247 while Uzbeks and Russians comprise 14.1% and 10.7% respectively (UN 2003: 39).

2 The International Crisis Group reports *Kyrgyzstan: After the Revolution* (2005a) and *Kyrgyzstan: A Faltering State* (2005b) provide a good introduction to events in Kyrgyzstan leading up to the March 24 overthrow of Akaev and his government and in the aftermath.

3 The following newspapers have been used to trace public discourses of "security" and related securising moves/securitisations: In Bishkek: *Slovo Kyrgyzstana, Vechernii Bishkek, MSN, ResPublica, Obshchestvenniy reiting, Belyj parakhod, Novyj Kyrgyzstan*. In Osh: *Vechernii Bishkek, MSN, ResPublica* (all when available), *Ekho Osha, Itogi nedeli*.

4 http://www.fti.org.kg/eng/_op_main.php [last accessed 01/02/2007]

5 I discuss one such example in section 3. See also Wilkinson 2007b.

6 By contrast, for example, if I had attempted to conduct research in a rural area, then Russian would have been largely useless. The decision to use Russian was determined by the precise circumstances of the research being undertaken – and, it should be noted, the research focus was in no small part determined by Russian being a suitable language for the field and known by the researcher, partly as a result of her having previously studied Russian in Kyrgyzstan.

7 The most violent incident in Kyrgyz-Uzbek relations was the "Osh conflict" that occurred in June 1990, when interethnic riots broke out in Uzgen and resulted in, according to different estimates, between 100 and 300 deaths. For a fuller account and analysis of the conflict, see Tishkov, 1995.

8 The double hermeneutic is a theory developed by Anthony Giddens (1977) that the relationship between everyday concepts and social science concepts is two-way, i.e. they both influence and affect each other.

[9] Collectively, the School is represented by the following works: Buzan, 1991; Wæver et al., 1993; Wæver 1995; Buzan, Wæver and de Wilde, 1998; and Buzan and Wæver, 2003.

[10] For a fuller explanation of the mechanism of securitisation, see Wæver et al., 1993: 23-26.

[11] Due to the importance of personal relationships in Kyrgyzstan, I draw a distinction here between personal contacts (i.e. people whom I had already met and knew personally from previously being in Bishkek) and contacts with whom I had no prior direct personal relationship, but who were known to me, and I to them, via colleagues. As I discovered, the two categories have very different "rules of engagement".

[12] Interview with V. Tyupin, chair of NGO Oazis, Bishkek, 26 Nov 2005

[13] Interview with member of NGO Labrys, Bishkek, 14 December 2005.

[14] Interview with members of Kel-Kel youth organisation, Bishkek, 22 November 2005.

[15] The Copenhagen School recognises that societal and political identities are likely to be interlinked, but argues that they are distinct from "the explicitly political organisations concerned with government" in that "society is about identity, the self-conception of communities and of individuals identifying themselves as members of a community" (Buzan, Wæver and de Wilde, 1998).

[16] Prior to March 25, 2005, Feliks Kulov had been serving a seven-year prison sentence following his conviction in January 2001 for alleged abuse of his position as a serving army officer. The charges were widely believed to be politically motivated since Kulov was seen to be a growing threat to the then-incumbent president, Askar Akaev. Ryspek Akmatbaev claimed that whilst in prison Kulov established links with Chechen mafia authority Aziz Batukaev.

[17] See FTI/IFES Early Warning for Violence Prevention Bulletins No. 17 and 18.

[18] Land ownership reform has been a long-running problem in Kyrgyzstan. People began seizing land on the outskirts of Bishkek in early 2005 in response to the government's failure to implement reforms throughout the previous 15 years.

[19] Interview with Rozmukhamet Akhmetovich Abdulbakiev, Chairman of the Uighur Association Ittipak, 19 December 2005.

[20] Interview with members of Kel-Kel youth organisation, Bishkek, 22 November 2005.

[21] Interview with V. Tyupin, chair of NGO Oazis, Bishkek, 26 Nov 2005

[22] Thanks to the anonymous reviewer who commented on this phenomenon.

[23] This separating of two of my identities may seem artificial to many. However, I make it here to emphasise that my efforts to place myself in a subordinate position were done with reference to my Researcher identity – for example, highlighting that I wished to learn from my interviewee, placing myself in a pupil role verbally and physically – rather than in reference to any performance of stereotypical feminine (and by extension subordinating) behaviour. This distinction is largely grounded in my being someone who does not personally identify (except from social necessity) with the label "woman" beyond a purely biological level, nor with binary gender constructs. How my interviewee interpreted my actions, however, is open to question.

[24] See Halberstam's (1998) discussion of the "bathroom problem" [getting mistaken for a man in the women's bathroom] (20-29), which very much reflects my personal experiences.

[25] One of the best illustrations of how naïve the sort of questions members of the LGBT community often get asked by well-intentioned straight people is the Heterosexuality Quiz. Devised by M. Rochlin in 1982, it poses a list of questions such as "What do you think caused your heterosexuality?" and "To whom have you disclosed your heterosexuality? How did they react?" It is now sometimes used to facilitate thinking about heteronormativity, or issues of unearned privilege more widely. See www2.kenyon.edu/Depts/Projects/Wmns21/actlinks.htm [last accessed 01/02/2007]

[26] A sensibility could be created by an explicit awareness of how any aspect of one's personality affects one's perception of the surrounding world. I would argue, however, that is likely to be a personal and emotive aspect rather than a purely objective characteristic in that it has affected one's experiences and is likely to be at odds with the prevailing societal norms – for example, a feminist sensibility or an immigrant sensibility in relation to one's old and new countries.

# References

Angrosino, Michael V. (1986) 'Son and lover: The anthropologist as nonthreatening male.' In: Tony Larry Whitehead and Mary Ellen Conway (eds) *Self, sex and gender in cross-cultural fieldwork*. University of Illinois Press, Urbana and Chicago, pp 64-83

Bayard de Volo, Lorraine and Edward Schatz (2004) 'From the inside out: Ethnographic methods in political research.' *PS: Political Science & Politics* 37(2):267-271

Behnke, Andreas (2000) 'The message or the messenger? Reflections of the role of security experts and the securitization of political issues.' *Cooperation and Conflict* 35(1):89-105

Bishop, Wendy (1992) 'I-witnessing in composition: Turning ethnographic data into narratives.' *Rhetoric Review* 11(1):147-158

Buzan, Barry, (1991) *People, states and fear*. Second edition. Harvester Wheatsheaf, Hemel Hempstead

Buzan, Barry, Ole Wæver and Jaap de Wilde (1998) *Security. A new framework for analysis*. CO: Lynne Rienner Publishers, London and Boulder

Buzan, Barry and Ole Wæver (1997) 'Slippery? Contradictory? Sociologically untenable? The Copenhagen School replies.' *Review of International Studies* 23:241-250

Buzan, Barry and Ole Wæver (2003) *Regions and powers*: Cambridge University Press, Cambridge

Doty, R.L. (2004) 'Maladies of our souls: identity and voice in the writing of academic international relations.' *Cambridge Review of International Affairs* 17(2):377-392

England, Kim V.L. (1994) 'Getting personal: reflexivity, positionality, and feminist research.' *Professional Geographer* 46(1):80-89

Eriksson, Johan (1999a) 'Observers or advocates? On the political role of security analysts.' *Cooperation and Conflict* 34(3):311-330

Eriksson, Johan (1999b) 'Debating the politics of security studies. Response to Goldmann, Wæver and Williams.' *Cooperation and Conflict* 34(3):345-352

Goldmann, Kjell (1999) 'Issues, not labels, please! Reply to Eriksson.' *Cooperation and Conflict* 34(3):331-333

Gonzalez, Nancie L. (1986) 'The anthropologist as female head of house-hold.' In: Tony Larry Whitehead and Mary Ellen Conway (eds.) *Self, sex and gender in cross-cultural fieldwork.* University of Illinois Press Urbana and Chicago, pp 84-100

Goodman, Liz (1996) 'Rites of passing.' In: Ellen Lewin and William L. Leap (eds.) *Out in the field.* University of Illinois Press, Urbana and Chicago, pp 49-57

Halberstam, Judith (1998) *Female masculinities.* Duke University Press, Durham, NC

International Crisis Group (2005a) *Kyrgyzstan: after the revolution.* Asia Report 97, 4 May 2005

International Crisis Group (2005b) *Kyrgyzstan: a faltering state.* Asia Report 109, 16 December 2005

Khan, Shahnaz (2005) 'Reconfiguring the native informant: positionality in the global age.' *Signs: Journal of Women in Culture and Society* 30(4):2017-2035

Kunda, Gideon (1992) 'Appendix: methods – A confessional of sorts.' In: Gideon Kunda (ed.) *Engineering culture: control and commitment in a high tech corporation.* Temple University Press, Philadelphia, pp 229-240

Lewin, Ellen and William L. Leap (eds.) (1996) *Out in the field.* University of Illinois Press, Urbana and Chicago

Lynch, Cecelia (2005) 'The "R" word, narrative, and rerestroika.' In: Kristen Renwick Monroe (ed.) *Perestroika!: the raucous rebellion in political science.* Yale University Press, New Haven and London, pp 154-166

Mookherjee, Nayanika (2001) 'Dressed for fieldwork: sartorial borders and negotiations.' *Anthropology Matters Journal* URL: http://www. anthropologymatters.com/journal/2001/mookherjee_2001_dressed.htm (24/10/2006)

Newton, Esther (1996) 'My best informant's dress: the erotic equation in fieldwork.' In: Ellen Lewin and William L. Leap (eds.) *Out in the field.* University of Illinois Press, Urbana and Chicago, pp 212-235

Presser, L. (2005) 'Negotiating power and narrative in research: implications for feminist methodology.' *Signs: Journal of Women in Culture and Society* 30(4):2067-2090

Renwick Monroe, Kristen (ed.) (2005) *Perestroika!: the raucous rebellion in political science*. Yale University Press, New Haven and London

Roscoe, Will (1996) 'Writing Queer Cultures: An Impossible Possibility?' in Lewin, Ellen and William L. Leap (eds.) *Out in the Field*. University of Illinois Press, Urbana and Chicago, pp 200-211.

Shehata, Samer (2006) 'Ethnography, identity and the production of knowledge.' In: Dvora Yanow and Peregrine Schwartz-Shea (eds.) *Interpretation and method*. M.E. Sharpe, New York and London, pp 244-263

Taureck, Rita (2006) 'Securitization theory and securitization studies.' *Journal of International Relations and Development* 9(1):53-61

Tishkov, Valery (1995) "'Don't kill me, I'm a Kyrgyz!': An anthropological analysis of violence in the osh ethnic conflict.' *Journal of Peace Research* 32(2):133-149

UN (2003) *Common country assessment Bishkek: the UN system in Kyrgyzstan*. URL: http://www.undp.kg/english/publications/2003/2005110701.pdf

Wæver, Ole, Barry Buzan, Morten Kelstrup and Pierre Lemaitre (1993) *Identity, migration and the new security agenda in Europe*. St. Martin's Press, New York

Wæver, Ole (1995) 'Securitization and Desecuritization.' In: Ronnie D. Lipschutz (ed.) *On security*. Columbia University Press, New York, pp 46-86

Wæver, Ole (1999) 'Securitizing sectors? Reply to Eriksson.' *Cooperation and Conflict* 34(3):334-340

Wafer, James (1996) 'Out of the closet and into print: Sexual identity in the textual field.' In: Ellen Lewin and William L. Leap (eds.) *Out in the field*. University of Illinois Press, Urbana and Chicago, pp 261-273

Wax, Rosalie H. (1986) 'Gender and age in fieldwork and fieldwork education: 'Not any good thing is done by one man alone'.' In Tony Larry Whitehead and Mary Ellen Conway (eds.) *Self, sex and gender in cross-cultural fieldwork*. University of Illinois Press, Urbana and Chicago, pp 129-150

Williams, Michael C. (1999) 'The practices of security: critical contributions. reply to Eriksson.' *Cooperation and Conflict* 34(3):341-344

Williams, Walter L. (1996) 'Being gay and doing fieldwork.' In: Ellen Lewin and William L. Leap (eds.) *Out in the field.* University of Illinois Press, Urbana and Chicago, pp 70-85

Wilkinson, Claire (2007a) 'The Copenhagen School on tour in Kyrgyzstan: is securitization theory usable outside Europe?' *Security Dialogue* 38(1):5-25

Wilkinson, Claire (2007b) *You say 'security', we say 'safety': speaking and talking security in Kyrgyzstan.* Paper presented at the conference Methodologies in Peace Research held at the Centre for Peace Studies, University of Tromsø, Norway, in cooperation with the Tampere Peace Research Institute (TAPRI), Finland, 21-23 March 2007

Whitehead, Tony Larry and Mary Ellen Conway (eds) (1986) *Self, sex and gender in cross-cultural fieldwork.* University of Illinois Press, Urbana and Chicago

Yanow, Dvora (2006) *Reading as method: interpreting interpretations.* Paper presented at the workshop on Political Ethnography: What Insider Perspectives Contribute to the Study of Power, University of Toronto, Toronto, Canada, 26-28 October 2006

Yanow, Dvora and Peregrine Schwartz-Shea (2006) *Interpretation and method.* M.E. Sharpe, New York and London

# 4

## *Cultivating Fields of Knowledge*

### The problem of knowledge transfer in field research on land use in Burkina Faso

### Katrin Gleisberg

## 1. Introduction

This chapter draws upon the experience of an ongoing ZEF research in *Assessing land use and land cover change in south-western Burkina Faso: a multi-agent approach*. The research intends to investigate socio-economic, biophysical and political determinants causing land use and land cover changes in the Ioba province in south-western Burkina Faso as well as to assess these changes by applying a multi-agent system. In order to find determinants of land use and land cover changes at the regional level a household survey and a plot-based survey were conducted in three villages. Due to cultural differences, differences in language, educational level between the farmers and myself, and the number of households interviewed I was not able to conduct all interviews by myself. From the very beginning of my research, I was aware of the need for local field assistants. Apart from bridging the language divide between me and the local population, I expected the field assistants to serve as a pool for local knowledge that could help to prepare the survey and to adapt my field methodology to local conditions. However, the cooperation with local field assistants turned out to be difficult for several reasons including being an educated white woman with another cultural and social background.

Participation of local residents and the application of participatory research methods are usually seen as an appropriate way to take into account local processes and perspectives as well as to explore local knowledge and perceptions. Moreover, participatory methodologies allow generating both qualitative and quantitative information (Cornwall and Jewkes, 1995). Going through the literature of participatory research, I found numerous publications on user participation and community-based participation. The idea explored in that literature was how the research subjects, such as farmers or villagers, may participate actively in the research and have this way a voice reflected in the results. Although local interviewers also participate actively in research and shape its results, the literature provides only little advice for researchers involving local residents as interviewers in developing countries (e.g. Chambers, 1994). In this chapter, I describe and reflect the unexpected difficulties that I faced during recruiting, training and employing local interviewers as well as the knowledge divide within the research team, which occurred and turned out to be a serious challenge for the research.

## 2. Field survey design and the need for local assistance

The survey aimed to collect all relevant data to investigate socio-economic, biophysical and political determinants causing land use and land cover changes in the Ioba province in south-western Burkina Faso. Therefore, 30% of the households of three villages and 50% of the households within a Water User Association in Dano were selected to explore a representative sample. The survey consists of three parts including a household survey and two plot-based surveys containing information that are specific to land use in rainy season and in dry season, for which 468 interviews were conducted in total. The household survey and the first plot-based survey covering data on the dry season were conducted during a period of six months in the rainy season in 2006. The household survey basically aimed to collect data on the demographic structure of the households, housing conditions, the main occupations of household members, revenues, production assets, livestock keeping, and agricultural extension services. The plot-based survey carried out with the same households included questions on land use practice, access to land, labour as well as yields for the dry season 2005/ 2006. The survey was very labour intensive and time consuming for the field assistants and I had to visit all the land holdings of the selected households to take GPS points on every field.

Because the villages under investigation extend over a huge area and have very scattered settlements we had to cover long distances between households and land holdings of the households. Therefore, the second survey was conducted by two persons per household; one assistant asked the questions and filled out the questionnaire while the second assistant took the GPS points. The second plot-based survey capturing data specific to the rainy season was conducted in a three month period at the end of the dry season in 2007.

There were several reasons for involving local residents as interviewers. Firstly, the development of an appropriate questionnaire required local knowledge, for both the subject and the geographic area were rather unknown to me before arriving in the field site. Not all necessary knowledge on local conditions could be gained from the existing literature, which I had studied during the preparation period. This included knowledge about local concepts of time, distance and weight as well as names of agricultural tools and local land use practice. Second, research should be conducted in a respectful manner. Therefore, it was helpful to be advised by local residents while looking for suitable study sites in how to get access to the communities, how to introduce myself to the communities under investigation, and how to behave in front of local authorities and farmers. Third, the language divide had to be overcome. Although French is the official language in Burkina Faso, farmers in rural areas hardly speak it. Since I do not speak the local language of my study area, Dagara, I was neither able to conduct formal nor informal interviews in the villages without any assistance of a local translator. Finally, the high number of interviews that had to be conducted and the limited time frame for my field research required the employment of some field assistants.

## 3. Hiring and training the local colleagues

I aimed to work with six interviewers constantly during a period of five months. Because malaria is prevalent in the research area, I always had to take into account time lost due to illness in my planning. Therefore, the first idea was to recruit seven interviewers in case one of the field assistants fell ill. At the same time, two important questions arose: Where and how to find field assistants? The challenge to find suitable field assistants is well known but mostly only general recommendations are provided by research manuals, such as: one should hire professional interviewers, who stem from the same culture or ethnic group as the researched communities (see e.g. Bernard, 2002). These recommendations sound logical and appropriate. However, in practice it is difficult to find professional interviewers from the same ethnic group, particularly in West Africa where the educational level is low and the number of ethnic groups and local languages is almost uncountable. It is rather complicated to find professional interviewers in developing countries due to high illiteracy rates and insufficient educational systems, which request high costs for secondary and tertiary education. This is particularly true for Burkina Faso where the illiteracy rate is about 80%. Although there are a lot of national and international development agencies trying to involve and train local residents in their research and development projects, the number of so-called professionals is small. Nor is having professionals *necessarily* desirable, they too bring biases associated with their urban and educational background.

Before starting to recruit interviewers, I prepared a check list including skills and qualities which I wanted the interviewers to have; it included experiences in interviewing, the ability to communicate very well in the local languages, at least 6 years of schooling, and Dagara origin. For the initial recruitment I asked the local administrator of the Dreyer Foundation in Dano to help me find some suitable interviewers fitting my expectations. The first idea was to hire students studying sociology at the University of Ouagadougou with some experience in conducting interviews since working with experienced interviewers has numerous benefits in terms of time and reliability. The head of the faculty of sociology selected three students who were experienced in conducting interviews due to previous project employment in the context of international development cooperation.

It was apparent in the first meeting with the sociologists that they had their own idea of interviewing and of their role as interviewers. Certainly, it was interesting to listen to their suggestions about the definition of households and to learn about their perceptions of being an interviewer from the capital. Whereas I tended to become an insider regarding farmers' knowledge on land use, they insisted on their position as outsiders, i.e. they were not interested in informal discussions with farmers to complete knowledge on land use and to bridge the knowledge gap between them and the farmers. This became apparent when we had a discussion about the location where interviews should take place. The sociologists suggested conducting the interviews in the market place with household chiefs. I wanted the assistants to go to the compounds and households for certain reasons. There were several questions that could be easily answered by observing the households' environment. Additionally, some questions related to domains of women could not be answered by household chiefs. Above all, coming from the capital the students were not interested in staying for a longer period of time in a rural or peri-urban area. Finally and most crucial, it turned out that none of the three spoke the local language Dagara which clearly disqualified them for the work, in my opinion.

As a result, I decided to refuse the collaboration with them and to recruit instead local residents as interviewers. I was aware that I had to cut down with my expectations, in particular considering working experience, but inexperience was intended to be compensated by an intensive training and practical exercises. I asked once more the local administrator of the Dreyer Foundation to find some local residents, speaking fluent Dagara, and able to read and to write. Finally, we found four secondary school pupils willing to learn and to conduct the interviews. It was possible to hire pupils at least for a period of four months because of the long vacation time in the rainy season. For additional interviewers I managed to attract others via personal ties with the ones I had already recruited. As a result I had eight potential interviewers although this meant that there was no real selection of interviewers.

To work with assistants stemming from the same culture or ethnic group as the researched communities may also be beneficial for they can provide knowledge on their culture, perceptions, and traditions. In Dano, where the interviewers were recruited, the Dagara constitute the majority of the population. Aside from the Dagara, there live also other ethnic groups such as Mossi and Peulh[1]. Most locals affiliated to ethnic groups other Dagara are able to communicate in Dagara, particularly when they have grown up in Dano. Dagara was the only ethnic group in the villages under investigation; consequently, I wanted to work with Dagara natives. As mentioned above, I asked the local administrator of the Dreyer Foundation in Dano to find some suitable local residents. Since he is a Mossi, he introduced not only Dagara but also two Mossi to me. This can be interpreted as proof that family as well as ethnic affiliation play a crucial role in the allocation of jobs in Burkina Faso. Furthermore, a Peulh was recommended by another researcher. Later in the survey period, a second Peulh became member of our research team. The four non-Dagara fulfilled all the criteria including fluency in Dagara but it was still unknown whether the Dagara farmers would consider them as insiders. Despite of their affiliation to other ethic groups, I decided to work with them for several reasons.

Firstly, and most important to me, they turned out to be very loyal and more trustworthy than the four Dagara assistants. Secondly, since most of the time the assistants had to work in pairs, I tried to group a Dagara and a non-Dagara to avoid difficulties that a different ethnic affiliation might potentially cause. Thirdly, particularly at the beginning of the survey, I observed that they worked more seriously than the Dagara interviewers. Certainly, I have to admit that I could hardly control the interviews because of the language problem but from my perspective, I could not see any differences in the performance of interviewing between the Dagara and their non-Dagara colleagues. Fourthly, all assistants are embedded in the community of Dano. Their life is very similar in using the same tools and means of production which display similarity with all farmers in the villages under investigation. Agriculture is still important for the population of Dano though it is an urban area. Therefore, all of them were familiar with agricultural activities – an essential requirement to understand the questionnaires as well as the responses the farmers gave in order to avoid knowledge disparities between assistants and farmers. Finally, the Mossi and the Peulh worked faster and more accurately in terms of filling out the questionnaire as well as paying attention to control questions.

The initial selection and training session lasted more than two weeks. The participants' level of interviewing skills varied. Whereas six assistants were inexperienced, two of them had previous interviewing experience, even in Dagara villages. I intended to involve both of them in the training procedure to teach the others interviewing techniques. During the first day, participants were provided with background information on the aim of the research, the existing academic and my individual knowledge on local land use as well as general instructions for interviewing. Although I tried to explain in simple words what the research is about and despite the fact that simplicity was enhanced through my far from perfect French language skills at that time, I noticed that they had difficulties to follow my presentation. Following the introduction, I instructed the interviewer in their roles and responsibilities. For this I prepared one page manuals using simple words and short sentences. Again, I noticed that they had problems to understand.

Now it was high time for me to engage in finding a solution for this problem but I was at my wits end. At the beginning the assistants had not the heart to express their opinions or to ask questions when they could not grasp the idea. I figured that the schooling system which does not allow them to express their opinion, to criticise the teacher or to make suggestions was at the heart of the problem. I asked too much of them when I wanted to know their questions and suggestions to the questionnaires and to fieldwork. Therefore, I had to teach them not only in interviewing but also in asking questions concerning understanding. As one way to create a relaxed atmosphere I decided to play games with the assistants, especially role-plays that could teach them interviewing techniques. However, learning by playing was a new experience for the assistants. It was difficult to explain what everybody had to do and what the aim of the game was. Moreover, we had to overcome their efforts to avoid being the first player. To facilitate the procedure of the player selection and to reach a higher degree of interactivity we applied some tools, i.e. a ball. I asked one of the experienced assistants to take the part of the farmer and to throw a ball to the person who should ask one question of the questionnaire. After a short while all of them understood what they have to do and soon they really enjoyed the role-plays.

Since they were not used to role-plays it was rather easy for the assistants to get into the game and to create team spirit. Playing games definitely contributed to creating a more relaxed atmosphere in terms of learning but less so in terms of expressing opinions. Nevertheless playing games was worthwhile for several reasons. First of all it was an appropriate way to learn how to ask questions and how to react to farmers' answers and behaviour. Moreover, I could detect their strength and weaknesses and adapt the training accordingly. Through analyzing the assistants' way of asking and answering I noticed which questions or terms in the questionnaires were not clear yet. Sometimes they provided the solution to the problems without knowing when they explained the question to their game-partners. I became aware of the variety of possibilities to interpret a question and could decide what interpretation to take to record the desired data. In cases where my assistants were not able to express what was unclear I had to come up with different possible interpretations from which they chose the one fitting most to local understanding.

Most interviewing techniques the assistants learned through role-plays. Apart from communication skills the performance of the interviews required also some other abilities. Therefore, the initial training included also two days of practical exercises for the plot-based questionnaire. Conducting this questionnaire required the utilisation of a GPS device, a measuring tape and the use of prepared photographs for the determination of the types of soil and vegetation as well as different local methods of soil conservation. The use and ability to handle a GPS device was an impressive tool for the assistants. They were fascinated by the GPS device because electronic devices are still rare in Dano. Using the GPS device made them proud because the number of people knowing about GPS in Dano is very limited. Therefore, working with a white researcher and knowing about GPS was appropriate to enhance their prestige within the community of Dano. Within half a day they knew how to use the GPS device. In contrast, teaching them how to use the measuring tape and how to integrate the photographs during the interviews took two days even though they were familiar with the local soils and vegetation.

The interviewing skills of the participants improved considerably; however, after two weeks of intensive training a practical interviewing exercise turned out to be a disaster and raised substantial doubts about my own teaching skills. All of them had difficulties to fill out the questionnaires and I noticed that they had still difficulties in understanding some questions on the form. After some more practical interviewing exercises, there was only one person who did not progress and who I was wary of to take into the team. Finally, because of the above mentioned difficulties in recruiting suitable assistants the person was incorporated into the group. To ensure reliable data collection this person always had to work with one of the best assistants or under my personal guidance.

For the period of the survey we had irregular training sessions to evaluate the previous interviews and to discuss the organisation and performance of upcoming interviews. Besides I had to continue recruitment and training of interviewers during field work due to a high interviewer turnover. Because of a limited time frame the period of training was reduced to four days consisting of two days teaching theory and methodology and two days of practical training. I anticipated, once they were trained, I would work with the field assistants for the entire duration of the survey. However, only four of eight participants from the initial training course completed the survey until the end. The relatively high interviewer turnover had several reasons. Most of my assistants were students and two of them left Dano to enter a school in another city and four of them participated in short-term training. In addition, I needed periodic replacement for assistants who fell ill or had to take an exam. As a result of their insufficient working performance and tensions within the group I had to dismiss three assistants. Though I gained experience and adapted to the local situation, my efforts in giving explanations and instructions did not show the expected results. Therefore, I decided to rely more on involving the employed assistants in order to facilitate and accelerate the process of training. Since the assistants often worked in pairs, newly recruited interviewers learnt from more experienced interviewers or were assisted in the field by myself.

## 4. Among colleagues? – Roles and hierarchy

I intended to work with the local assistants as good colleagues and to not take on roles of students and researcher, recruits and boss. However, I have to confess that I underestimated this challenge for several reasons. On the one hand, I was challenged by their perception of me as outsider, student and researcher. Before being able to collect data and to generate knowledge on land use, the knowledge within the research team had to be accumulated. On the other hand, I had difficulties to adapt my expectations to the working conditions in Burkina Faso. To become an 'insider' or rather an equal member of the team I wanted to present myself as someone who was there to learn. Moreover, I relied on the assistants' insider knowledge on local land use practice and culture to adapt the questionnaires to local conditions. Hence, I needed to find out about their concept of time, weight, distance as well as local names of production and household means, and places. Additionally and even more important to me, I wanted them to teach me local rules of behaviour and conversation to carry out my research in a respectful manner. The turning-upside-down of roles in this case, becoming the student, they being teachers, was hard to put across.

The assistants often perceived me as team leader or researcher, who was expected to prepare all the means they needed, to give clear instructions and have solutions ready for all difficulties we would face during fieldwork. This became very apparent when we had an argument within the research team at the end of a working week. The Dagara assistants decided to refuse to continue the work when I told them that I am not satisfied with the completion of questionnaires and that I would not pay the full salary for the week since there was work for more than three days left. One the one hand, I wanted to show the assistants that I would not accept a steady inaccuracy. On the other hand, I paid a salary high above the national average. I wanted them to understand that they have to work for their salary since they considered me often as infinite source of money able and willing to pay for everything. Additionally, the assistants had arguments about responsibilities and allocation of work within their small groups of two. Being aware that they do not consider me as part of their group I perceived them as a group probably because I considered them as insider and all of them considered me as outsider. Therefore, I anticipated that all team members would contribute to solve the conflicts and encouraged them also to find solutions for their problems themselves.

Yet I have to admit that I underestimated the complexity of the group. They were not able to solve their conflicts and ask me to take decisions instead, which definitely showed that they did not accept me as an equal member of the team but as researcher and boss. Finally I decided to give all members of the team including myself the possibility to express annoyance and concerns within a group discussion and face to face discussions. Unfortunately, neither in the time-consuming group discussion nor in face to face discussions we found a solution that pleased everybody. The most crucial and emotional decision I had to make was to fire three assistants. On the one hand, this led to a loss of faith in my skills as their team leader amongst the team as well as a loss of faith in their ability to cooperate. In this situation, they perceived me definitely as their boss since to fire somebody from the team exercises the power of that position. On the other hand, this led to more loyalty particularly of the non-Dagara-assistants and to a closer collaboration with all remaining assistants.

Although they anticipated that I coordinate the field work and prepare all the means we need for the fieldwork, they never considered this activities as work because they could neither estimate the time effort nor overview my activities completely. As one way to bridge the researcher–assistant divide I intended to put more responsibility on the assistants and to involve them in data entry in addition to interview-taking. The idea was that showing the assistants what happens to the data they collected would further contribute to a more careful data generation. This plan proved to be too ambitious and time-consuming for me, mainly due to their inexperience with computers.

Except from the distinction between me as researcher and assistants as non-scientists, my white skin colour made me stand out of the group. Though they knew my name, of course, most of the time they called me "*Nassara*", the *mòoré*[2] word for whites, which clearly defined me as outsider of the group. The assistants presumed that I would not be able to do labour intensive or physically hard work. They did not anticipate me to conduct fieldwork together with them all day long. According to their assumptions, which are probably a result of the usual behaviours of whites who came to work in the region or some fuzzy ideas about white people, they thought I would not be capable to work in the field an equal amount of time. However, their belief that white people spend most of their time in air-conditioned houses or vehicles was corroborated when I had to coordinate the interviews or to enter data in my office. Although I tried to engage in their activities as much as I could, the hierarchy maintained since I was accommodated with other foreigners. Regarding this, I have never been an insider or rather an equal team member. Hence, I made efforts to become an equal team member through spending a lot of time with the assistants after work, showing interest and even actively participating in their daily life. The exchange of everyday issues contributed to a better understanding of local conditions and satisfied my curiosity how local residents cope with their daily lives. Conversely I tried to satisfy the curiosity of the assistants by telling them about daily life in Germany and my perceptions of Burkina Faso. At the end I was still *Nassara* but the divide between the assistants as insiders and me as outsider was considerably shrinking by that time.

Although they enjoyed teaching me about their life, their environment and what they consider as correct behaviour in our free-time, they had not really accepted me as a 'student' of theirs during the training period and fieldwork. This was also caused by the difference in age. Because all of them were secondary school students they were rather young and had no experience in teaching somebody who was about ten years older. In Burkina Faso, showing respect for people who are older is manifested by not answering them back and not lecturing them; but our roles were reversed. This further contributed to the assistants' perception of me as teacher and made it difficult for them to accept me as a student.

They taught not only me, they often taught each other as well. As mentioned above there was a high interviewer turnover and I had to continue the recruitment of interviewers in the survey period. During training sessions some experienced assistants taught the newcomers in role-plays how to react to farmers' behaviour and how to ask questions. Putting the responsibility for the training on assistants was beneficial for some reasons. Because the assistants knew what difficulties in understanding and what questions they had during the initial training course they could emphasise these issues better than I could. Additionally, as observer of the training I noticed uncertainties and difficulties in comprehension for the teaching assistants as well as for the newcomers from another perspective as that one of a trainer. The questionnaire contained several questions, which seemed to be not clear for them. Regarding this, the assistants had an essential influence on the design of the questionnaires. It turned out that some questions were rather diffuse. My observations made me think about what I actually wanted to know by asking these questions and how I wanted to define the subjects of these questions. The questionnaire contained for example questions on grain storages. For the assistants grain storage included granaries as well as sacks whereas I wanted to know only about granaries because I had not considered a sack as grain storage. Because sacks seemed to be grain storages for the local residents I had to think about how to include sacks in my considerations on grain storage. We discovered various misunderstandings like the given example during training courses and by solving them I learned a lot about local perceptions and attitudes.

Occasionally it turned out to be more appropriate to use expressions in Dagara since they seemed to be more precise than a long French explanation. The local concept of time, for example, refers to the position of the sun.

Because the villagers sometimes do not know the western concept of time with weeks, hours and minutes, it was essential to know about this concept to record time related data. This is also true for the concept of distance and weight. I did not know very well the Dagara expressions or local concepts. However, the assistants knew these concepts and how to apply them during the interviews.

## 5. Conclusion

It became obvious to me that data collection in the field may be confronted with severe problems of different fields of knowledge and a communication gap as well as with challenges of role changes. When reading other people's work, I sometimes think that this part of field research is not given appropriate attention. The optimal use of knowledge disparities between local assistants and external researcher requires pragmatic solutions to bridge the divide by actively getting engaged in the cultivation of the different fields of knowledge. Whilst the work and decision-making in the field is often ad hoc and decided by the situational context – and therefore often rather "sub-optimal", a critical reflection on the subject of cooperation between two field periods or after field research should be part of all research in the development context, also in cases when the divide seems less severe than in my own research, e.g. when researchers work with assistants in their home country.

My experiences suggest that integrating participatory aspects into the field research framework has methodological and practical implications for the research. Ultimately, practical considerations seemed to be more important. At the beginning of the field research my expectations regarding the involvement of local interviewers were far from being realistic. Apart from the difficulties in finding the right colleagues I overestimated their abilities and skills, and I misjudged the cooperation as well. Finally, the timeframe for training and fieldwork was not appropriate since training had to be extended. Despite the problems described here, employing local residents as interviewers was a worthwhile experience. The involvement of the assistants in the preparation of the interviews substantially contributed to successful data collection and provided me with deeper insights into local conditions.

## Notes

[1] English: Fulani or Fulbe

[2] Mòoré is the language of the Mossi.

## References

Bernard, H.R. (2002) *Research methods in anthropology: qualitative and quantitative approaches.* 3rd edition. AltaMira Press, Walnut Creek, CA

Chambers, R. (1994) 'Participatory rural appraisal (PRA): Analysis of experience.' *World Development* 22 (9):1253-1268

Cornwall, A. and Jewkes, R. (1995) 'What is participatory research?' *Social Science and Medicine* 41:1667-1676

5

# *The Best of Both Worlds*

## Integrating quantitative and qualitative approaches in forest management research in Indonesia

### Charles Palmer

*"…science consists in grouping facts so that general laws or conclusions may be drawn from them." (Charles Darwin)*

## 1. Introduction

The finding and grouping of Darwin's 'facts' may be more difficult to undertake in the social sciences than in the so-called 'hard sciences'. The growth in social scientific literature over recent decades along with the emergence of numerous sub-disciplines through interdisciplinary collaboration, e.g. environmental anthropology, development economics, while illustrating the vibrancy of social science research also underlines the lack of consensus in understanding what drives human behaviour. As knowledge is accumulated, the complexity of human societies and their interactions with one another and the natural world becomes ever more apparent.

Illustrated with examples from my own field research in Indonesia, this chapter is concerned with the types of methods used to collect data in the context of developmental and environmental policy in the developing world. Two of the biggest challenges for researchers are in formulating effective and efficient research approaches to survey design and sampling in the production of meaningful datasets given time and budgetary constraints. Fieldwork conditions in a developing country context typically demand a flexible approach to fieldwork. For the most part, the research methods chosen will be conditional on the researcher's background (discipline), training and experience. In this chapter, I broadly classify approaches according to whether they are quantitative or qualitative, with the former relying more on quantitative data, i.e. numbers, and statistical analysis and the latter more on qualitative data gathered from a 'case study', action research or more ethnographic approach.

From the perspective of reaching a predetermined research goal, a combined approach may be better than using one approach alone given a set research budget. Thus, I am in agreement with Onwuegbuzie and Leech (2005) that there is a need for students to develop into 'pragmatic researchers' through the combination of quantitative and qualitative methods in social science research. A pragmatic approach would require the selection of a set of methods that most adequately address the research question at hand. Much of the best analytical work that has been carried out in recent years utilises both statistical analysis and the case study approach. For example, a seminal paper by André and Platteau (1998) utilized an in-depth case study and statistical analysis to explore the linkages between land distribution and tenure arrangements, income opportunities and the tensions underlying the civil war in Rwanda. A recent review by Bryman (2006) shows some of the ways in which qualitative and quantitative research can be integrated, although without a focus on any particular area of research.

The question that follows is why emphasise a more integrated approach in the specific context of environment and development issues in developing countries? First, environment and development issues can only be understood in terms of linkages and trade-offs, particularly where poverty is ever-present (see for example, López, 1998). Thus, the choices made by policy-makers and households will reflect these trade-offs, which may not be apparent from observing selected cases in the field. These studies, nevertheless, can give valuable insights into local belief and customary systems and power relations, amongst other things. Quantitative data on land-use and natural resource degradation over a wider area may give more weight to the case study findings, or perhaps different insights altogether. Second, and on the other hand, over-reliance on data from a large sample of communities or households (whether government-collected or self-gathered) may lead to skewed or biased results if care is not taken to control for the variation in local conditions and cross-checking of the data is not undertaken. For example, property rights systems over land and natural resources are more likely to vary from one locale to the next in a developing country than in a developed country; this legal pluralism is often more prevalent in developing countries due to the parallel existence of statutory, customary and local law systems. Knowledge gained from a qualitative approach would help to correct for this kind of variation in the analysis. A third and final point is the demand for more integrated approach to research from research organisations and programmes in order to provide more credible policy advice to governments. In this chapter, for example, I detail a number of forest research studies, which have attempted such an integrated approach. Some of these have been undertaken in collaboration with the Center for International Forestry Research (CIFOR), an international organization that is planning to undertake more controlled, comparative studies involving data analysis than it ever did before (Capistrano, pers. comm.).

The remainder of this chapter is structured as follows. Section 2 presents the background to the themes explored. In section 3, I consolidate my experiences in conducting fieldwork in Indonesia, spanning almost five years between 2002 and 2006. In this section, I will describe my attempts at integrating qualitative and quantitative approaches to research and analysis. Section 4 presents a discussion of these attempts and potential ways forward for future research, and section 5 concludes.

## 2. Background

Research methods can be classified along a continuum according to how the research is undertaken and by the method in which the results are analysed. At one end of the continuum, 'qualitative' methods will refer to the 'case study' approach. While case studies in themselves usually utilise quantitative data in one form another, they may not use quantitative or statistical techniques for data analysis. Moreover, these quantitative data might be very local and perhaps not useful on a wider scale. For example Barr et al. (2001) provide an excellent case study of the impacts of decentralization within a small group of villages in one region of Indonesia. The numbers used in this single study are not 'typical' of a broader cross-section of Indonesian villages, an observation that was confirmed with the findings from a wider study (see Palmer, 2006). In exploring best practice for research methods, I will follow Boos (1992), where the 'case study' is frequently associated with the exploratory case study. This study usually precedes a final study, which can, itself, be a case study, but it can also have a different design. As Scholz and Tietje (2002) note, exploratory case studies can help to gain insight into the structure of a phenomenon in order to develop hypotheses, models or theories. This kind of study resembles a pilot study in which the research design and data collection methods are usually not specified in advance. Other types of case study and their applications are also described in Scholz and Tietje (2002). In environment and development research, the case study approach is commonly, though not exclusively, used by sociologists, political scientists and anthropologists.

At the other end of the continuum, 'quantitative' methods are ones in which data collection and the application of statistical methods are paramount, thus typically requiring the sampling of a large, representative number of cases, be they households, individuals, firms or nations. In the area of development research, quantitative methods are commonly used by economists, although they tend towards analyses either using government data or household field surveys. While there is relatively little in the way of practical guides on undertaking fieldwork with large samples in developing countries, Ethridge (2004) covers research methods in development economics with some guidelines on data collection.

Underlying both these approaches is the scientific method where techniques for investigating phenomena and acquiring new knowledge are developed. Crucially, these are based on observable, empirical (sometimes only partly) measurable evidence and subject to the laws of reasoning. Specific hypotheses are proposed as explanations of natural or social phenomena and studies, typically based on more quantitative than qualitative data, are designed that test these predictions for accuracy. These steps are repeated in order to make increasingly dependable predictions of future results (cause and effect), or to establish relations among variables (correlation). However, the process must be objective so that the researcher does not bias the interpretation of the results. Both types of research method are vulnerable to data manipulation and bias, and need to be undertaken with great care. Moreover, research results presented in certain ways can lead to differing interpretations. The job of the scientist, both natural and social, is to remain impartial to his or her subject and present the results in an unbiased manner, or at least reflect on the existing bias (which may have been unavoidable) in these and make them as transparent as possible to the reader.

In applications of the scientific method, including that concerning environment and development, the establishment of the so-called 'counterfactual' is important in setting up any research. In other words, what would have happened if the social phenomena under study, e.g. type of policy or environmental change, had not have happened (see Ferraro and Pattanayak, 2006). Ideally, one subset of any given sample will have been subject to the phenomenon under study with a control group not subject to this. This allows for a direct comparison of cases and the separation of effects on the variable of interest. In the real world of course, the counterfactual can be very difficult to establish, although methods have been and are continuing to be developed to deal with this issue (see for example, Ravallion, 2001). Good examples of research that have established the counterfactual and, in these cases, attempted to ascertain the effectiveness of environmental policy can be seen in recent work in Costa Rica, e.g. Sánchez-Azofeifa et al. (2003). Ignoring the counterfactual can lead to misinterpretations of data and a reinforcement of 'conventional wisdom', where people believe something because in some way it 'makes sense'. This is simply not scientific[1]. But, it should be stressed that any kind of comparison needs to be undertaken very carefully. The omission of certain variables (whether due to oversight or not), for example, can also lead to misleading results and onerous differences among a comparative sample of cases.

## 3. Examples of research methods from Indonesia

In this section, lessons will be drawn from four research studies undertaken in Indonesia between 2002 and 2006. In each case, I briefly describe the study's background and research objectives along with the reasoning behind these. This is followed by a discussion of the research methods used and the problems encountered in interpreting the fieldwork results.

### *Illegal logging and the logging trade*

In the late 1990s, illegal logging, in both developed and developing countries became a global issue due to its myriad social, economic and environmental implications (see for example, Callister, 1999). In 2002, I was contracted by CIFOR to develop a conceptual and empirical framework for defining 'illegal logging' and then to use this to quantify illegal timber flows in Indonesia. In addition to national level studies such as Scotland et al. (1999) and Palmer (2001), this research was motivated by previous work case studies undertaken by, for example, McCarthy (2000) and Telepak Indonesia and the Environmental Protection Agency (1999). All these studies indicated that the problem of illegal logging in Indonesia, however defined, had substantially worsened since the Asian financial crisis hit the economy followed by the collapse of the authoritarian Suharto regime, during 1997-98.

CIFOR wanted a more accurate, regional quantitative analysis and a comparison of import/export log flow data between Indonesia and Malaysia. At that time, there existed a large amount of largely anecdotal evidence of timber smuggling from Indonesia to Malaysia and China, but little in the way of hard, quantitative data to show that this was indeed the case. Thus, CIFOR was keen to see hard evidence that timber illegally felled in Indonesia was being smuggled to Malaysia or China.

Between February and May 2002, I, along with CIFOR colleagues were set the task of developing a framework for quantifying timber flows from areas of production, to points of export, and from one Indonesian province to another and to international markets. Furthermore, we were to gather the necessary government data from offices at the provincial and district levels (the second and third tiers of Indonesian government, respectively). This was to allow us to compare data for timber movements from out of one area and into another. Thus, it was hoped that by tracking timber flows from production to processing we could analyse the data gaps and hence, the level of illegal (i.e. unlicensed) production in any given area. East Kalimantan province was selected as a test case due to CIFOR's previous fieldwork experience there. We also had a list of useful contacts that we could utilise in order to provide qualitative evidence to complement the government data. These included key 'forest stakeholders' such as timber traders, other industry representatives such as exporters and timber mill owners, and government officials working in the forestry and customs offices. Information already existed that showed that much timber from East Kalimantan was processed in East Java province and the state of Sabah in Malaysia. We planned to travel to these two areas to interview similar stakeholders, in addition to visiting and collecting government data from state- and provincial-level offices.

We prepared a quantitative framework, along the lines of a material flows analysis, for the data we hoped to collect, and a fieldwork plan for travelling through East Kalimantan, East Java and Sabah. Moreover, we prepared a semi-structured questionnaire for each type of stakeholder, although we allowed the discussions to be as open as necessary should they shed any further light on particular 'black market' issues relating to log flows e.g. payments of bribes, smuggling routes. Meetings were set up with our contacts as we travelled through all districts in East Kalimantan, visiting the forestry office in each one. Interviews were conducted in Indonesian and repeat appointments were made where possible when information needed to be clarified or further information was required. We also visited a number of government departments in the provincial capital, Samarinda, as well as the provincial capital of East Java, Surabaya. Interviews were held with stakeholders in most of the offices visited and government data were collected at both the district and provincial levels. We attempted to collect data on log production, processing, imports and exports. For corroboration, these data were gathered from both the statistics and forestry departments in Samarinda. In Sabah, we carried out more interviews and collected forestry data, particularly on log production, processing, imports and exports (of both raw logs and processed timber).

Overall, we were successful in data gathering but were ultimately unsuccessful in providing a clear quantitative picture of illegal log flows from the forests of Kalimantan to the timber mills of Sabah. Hence, we could not show, using quantitative data, that logs illegally cut in Indonesia were being smuggled to Malaysia. The quality of the data collected at both district and provincial levels in East Kalimantan were poor and inconsistent. Moving from one district to the next, it was very difficult to avoid double counting, and almost impossible to verify the numbers. However, it was clear from the dozens of interviews that we carried out that illegal logging was rife; log harvesting, processing and shipping took place on a large scale without the appropriate licenses. Furthermore, the corruption of government officials by timber traders to circumvent the rules was very common. The illicit nature of the trade naturally made a more objective sampling of forest stakeholders problematic.

Despite these problems, the Indonesian data were of reasonable enough quality to show that timber processing did not take place on a large scale in East Kalimantan despite the millions of cubic metres of logs being harvested there each year. Moreover, East Kalimantan export data showed that relatively few raw logs were officially exported in the time period under study. The data collected for Sabah, on the other hand, were of a much higher quality and it was shown that substantial gaps existed between official log imports, local log production and the amount of logs being used for processing. Forestry officials in Sabah acknowledged these gaps and stated that the bulk of raw logs used for processing originated from East Kalimantan. Nevertheless, this evidence was still not enough to show beyond reasonable doubt, the links between log production in East Kalimantan and log processing in Sabah.

## Impacts of decentralization on forest-dependent communities

There is a huge literature on the decentralization of natural resource management and the devolution of resource use and ownership rights to local user groups such as tribes and local communities (see for example, Agrawal and Ribot, 1999). Much of this focuses on the impacts of decentralization and devolution in social, economic and environmental terms, using the case study approach (for a recent review see, Larson and Ribot, 2004). Within this literature, there is also a body of theory on decentralization impacts, based on these studies. Much of collective action theory, for example, is based on case studies of community experiences of managing natural resources at the local level (see Ostrom, 1990; Baland and Platteau, 1996). While some researchers have attempted to compare cases, differences in research methods makes these comparisons largely general and in some cases, speculative. Assessing the impacts of decentralization has been beset with problems of definition (of impacts) and methodology in comparing one case to the next.

These problems are not confined to Indonesia alone, although given the huge scale of decentralization there in the late 1990s there has been a lot of research interest in assessing its impacts. In particular, forest sector decentralization enabled forest-dependent communities to claim forest use rights, which were negotiated away to logging firms in exchange for financial and in-kind benefits. Resosudarmo (2004) and Casson and Obidzinski (2002), for example, analysed the impacts of these changes on communities, mainly in financial and ecological terms. However, these studies were based on field observations from a limited set of cases that could not be extrapolated to a wider area. Thus, the challenge was to use these observations as the basis for the development of a suite of 'decentralization impacts' and hypotheses that could be tested with quantitative data collected from a larger sample of cases in the field.

Between 2002 and 2005, as part of my doctoral studies at the Center for Development Research (ZEF) in Bonn, I developed a framework for quantifying the impacts of forest sector decentralization on Indonesian communities using very narrow definitions of impact and of the groups concerned. I focused on communities that had negotiated logging agreements as a result of decentralization and had also experienced logging in their forest areas before decentralization. The 'community' was used as my unit of measurement, defined as a group of people that had negotiated a single agreement for the benefit of all members of that group. Members in the group were usually connected by family and ethnicity, and held a historical, customary forest claim. This was to allow for a direct comparison of experiences across communities. Guided by the results from a large number of previous case studies and decentralization theory, I identified five different, but related, categories of impact including financial and ecological ones, and hypothesised how decentralization might change these. Given time and budgetary constraints, these indicators were a combination of recollections and perceptions of changes.

Based on these indicators, I prepared questions for community- and household-level surveys, most of which followed a structured, 'closed' format, either with 'yes', 'no', and 'don't know' tick boxes or lists of possible answers plus tick boxes. I did not want to leave questions open to interpretation, which would make comparisons across households and communities problematic. The community survey was designed for the focus group discussions with community leaders who were typically the community members who had participated in the negotiations for a logging agreement. There were a large number of short questions in order to permit a discussion to move along in a structured manner. Of course while there was nothing to stop a discussion from moving away from a predetermined and logical sequence of questioning, the survey was structured to allow for this. For most questions, comments and open boxes were incorporated to allow the research team to gather extra information where available. The team was trained to systematically follow the structure of the surveys but to always be aware of and note extra information wherever possible. For the community survey they were trained to build questions into the discussion and to return to points that may have been missed along the way, thus ensuring that all questions were covered. The team was instructed to check that all questions were answered and not to 'put answers into the mouths of respondents'. It was emphasised that an answer of 'don't know' was as valid as any other. Where an answer did not correspond to anything on the survey, there was always an empty box marked 'other' for these. So, while it was imperative that the data be collected in such a way as to minimise researcher bias and subjective interpretation of data in order to allow for inter-community comparison, I wanted also wanted to pick up information that may not have been considered during the questionnaire design phase. For some communities, some basic community characteristics, e.g. on population, ethnicity etc, were cross-checked against data collected by other researchers in previous surveys. In general, the data we collected compared well to that which were collected in the past.

The household survey was far shorter and designed more for one-to-one question and answer sessions lasting up to an hour. While it was primarily designed for the head of a household, many of the questions were similar to those asked to village leaders and also followed a closed format. The household responses were to be used to corroborate community-level responses and to build community-level indices, e.g. for levels of financial benefits received.

With a research team of six local researchers, a pre-test of the surveys was followed by the random sampling of 65 communities and 687 households in East Kalimantan, in 2003-2004. Communities were sampled using lists of communities contained in previous research reports and from government offices. A large sample with at least 50-55 communities was required to enable the use of statistical techniques for the data analysis. The difficulties of travelling in East Kalimantan along with budget and time constraints meant that there was an element of selectivity bias in the results (see Palmer, 2006:47). Within each community, between six and 20 households were randomly sampled (according to the size of the community) using community lists of households typically held in the 'village office'.

The hypotheses were empirically tested using these data with the results fitting the hypotheses relatively well, as can be seen in Palmer (2006) and Palmer and Engel (2006). In these analyses quantitative and qualitative data were combined, with the qualitative data not only used to build community-level indices, e.g. levels and types of intra-community conflict over the distribution of logging fees, but also to map the networks of 'power relations' through East Kalimantan as well as other phenomena not so easily reduced to econometric analysis. The information on these networks helped to describe cartel-like behaviour among firms, which at least in part explained the patterns of negotiated logging fees observed across the province.

There were some issues with the research methods used in this study. First, the dependence on communities' perceptions of change for some indicators meant that for the purposes of comparing perceptions across communities I had to take care in how these questions were asked and in interpreting the answers. To try and get around this, the indicators used were kept very simple, asking respondents, for example, *whether* there had been a change in, for example, a particular environmental impact rather than by how much. The qualitative responses to these questions, similar to many in the household survey, were used to build up quantitative indices for the whole community. Ideally, with more time and money, the responses to these kinds of questions could have been qualified and perhaps answered more objectively, for example, by hiring people to carry out field assessments of actual environmental impacts from logging.

Second, in making a comparison of community experiences before and after decentralization, the survey asked respondents questions on events that had happened many years previously. In the absence of time-series data, these kinds of questions always run the risk of obtaining answers that have been contaminated with knowledge gained from having the benefit of hindsight. To counter this, the pre-decentralization section was kept as brief as possible. Moreover, like most of the rest of the survey, the questions dwelled less on attitudes, opinions and preferences and instead attempted to draw these out indirectly through data and information gathered on actual events and actions, with corroboration across the two surveys.

Third, the household samples in each community, while generally representative, were not as large as they perhaps should have been in some of the larger communities. Thus, some of the community-level indices may have been measured more accurately for the smaller communities compared to the larger ones.

Fourth, even with all the preparation beforehand, very little was really known about the situation on the ground until the fieldwork commenced. For instance, the lists of communities with logging agreements held by local governments were not always up to date or reliable. Thus, given the situation on the ground the research team were required to be flexible in how they approached the communities in the sample. They were issued with clear guidelines on how to approach communities given certain types of problem (see Palmer, 2006).

## *The factors underlying variation in outcomes from community-firm agreements*

In previous case studies, e.g. Barr et al. (2001), it was observed that wide variation existed in the financial and in-kind benefits that flowed to communities that had negotiated logging agreements with logging firms in Indonesia. These benefits have been observed to occur in many cases where local user groups received rights to use and manage natural resources (see Baland and Platteau, 1996). Nevertheless, relatively little was known about what actually explains this observed variation. Building on a game-theoretic model of community-firm interactions developed by Engel et al. (2006) and Engel and López (2004), hypotheses were derived regarding the factors that might influence the relative size of community payoffs. These can be seen in Engel and Palmer (2006).

The data for this research were collected during the same fieldwork phase described in the previous study. While the development of the survey questions followed the hypotheses mentioned in the previous paragraph, they were also tested during an 'exploratory case study' phase. The results from this case study can be seen in Palmer (2004). Afterwards, the mainly 'closed' community- and household-level surveys were finalised and the fieldwork organised as previously described. The survey data were used to form proxies that could be used in regression analysis. Again, the empirical analysis showed that the results approximately conform to the hypotheses (see Engel and Palmer, 2006; Palmer, 2006).

As in the previous study, the surveys sought to combine the collection of quantitative and qualitative data. The qualitative data, at the household level, were again primarily used to build community-level (quantitative) indices. Qualitative data collected during focus-group discussions with community leaders were used to form a narrative for each community as a whole and fill in the gaps where the quantitative data were unavailable or required qualification and explanation. I tried to ensure that the structure and composition of the questionnaires were both practical and rigorous. Taken together, the use of community level and household level questionnaires enabled me to corroborate the responses given. Where possible, the information gathered was cross-checked with other sources. In particular, details on the logging agreements were checked with the information that was available from district government, data collected from previous studies and extended informal discussions with the few community members who had worked for the logging firms.

I designed the surveys for a greater breadth of data and information, but at the cost of some depth. The use of many, short close-ended questions allowed for more direct comparisons across communities, although there was a danger that vital information might bypass the interviewers. To get around this problem, the research team was again encouraged to talk to as many people as possible in the relatively short time available in each community, and collect information that did not always fit comfortably into the survey format used. Nevertheless, it was perhaps inevitable that details will be lost in undertaking an approach of this kind, even accounting for the fact that it was always going to be impossible to observe everything that had occurred in the surveyed communities. Thus, the characteristics of communities were captured by quite approximate indicators, e.g. the use of government employment to proxy for opportunity costs. A more detailed (and costly) survey would aim to capture the variation in employment among communities and hence, allow for the formulation of more precise proxies.

From the fieldwork, however, it was clear that more detailed questions often resulted in misunderstandings among respondents, particularly ones that might be more locale-specific. While some questions could be adapted to local conditions, this required that the research team learn to understand the precise motivations behind these, which was not always possible. These questions subsequently failed to elicit the clear responses necessary to form more robust proxies for the regression analysis, which suggests that there may be limits to the quality and quantity of data that can be collected from the field. For example, a section towards the end of both surveys had a number of hypothetical 'what if' questions, which were to be used to gauge what respondents had learned from their logging experiences. Unfortunately, many people were unable to understand that these were not questions recollecting events of the past (unlike the remainder of the survey), and were subsequently dropped.

The considerable financial and logistic constraints on collecting quantitative data from a cross-section of communities limited the sample size and thereby the possibilities for a more detailed econometric analysis. While the empirical results reported in Engel and Palmer (2006) appears reasonably robust, high levels of collinearity among variables prevent separating out the effects of alternative factors influencing the broad parameters identified by the model.

### The effectiveness of community conservation agreements on land-use behaviour

Ferraro and Pattanayak (2006) argue that given limited resources for conservation, policy in this field needs to adopt state-of-the-art programme evaluation methods in order to improve policy design. In Lore Lindu National Park in Central Sulawesi, Indonesia, local communities with legitimate claims to forest areas were observed clearing forest for the establishment of commodity crops such as cocoa and coffee. In 1999 onwards, 'conservation agreements' were negotiated between local forest-dependent communities and the national park authorities in approximately 40 communities located close to the Park. These agreements were facilitated by various non-governmental organizations (NGOs), ranging from local to international ones such as the Nature Conservancy and Care International. Under these agreements communities committed to complying with specified conservation rules in return for defined forest use rights and some other benefits provided by the government and NGOs.

This study was established in December 2005 to update and upscale information on the establishment of community conservation agreements in communities surrounding the Park. Furthermore, the intention was to assess community behaviour regarding land use and extraction within the borders of the Park, and to identify and measure crucial characteristics of the communities (socio-economic, ecological, etc.) and of the established agreements (contract provisions, time of establishment, monitoring and enforcement, etc.). It was hoped that we could analyze the degree to which these characteristics explain the variation in observed community behaviour and related conservation outcomes. We would like to draw conclusions for the design of appropriate and effective policies to promote the sustainable use of Park resources. Mappatoba (2004) describes how agreements by some NGOs were more effective than others. Thus, by surveying agreements by different organizations, we hoped to test for effectiveness with respect to agreement type too.

Given these research objectives, I developed a community-level survey based on one that was undertaken by another group of researchers in 2001, which was to be undertaken in the same sample of communities surveyed in that year (see Zeller et al., 2002). Thus, the idea was to reproduce the 2001 survey and to include a new section on the community agreements. Approximately two-thirds of the sample had negotiated these agreements since the previous survey was undertaken. This will enable a comparison of community land-use behaviour, from 2001 until 2006, and between those that made agreements and those that did not. I hypothesised that communities that had made agreements were less likely to clear forest inside the Park than those not involved in agreements. Moreover, agreements made by some organizations were hypothesised to be more effective in managing community land-use decisions than others.

Survey design was guided by the 2001 survey, as well as the analysis that utilised these data (see Maertens, 2004). Articles such as those by Angelsen and Kaimowitz (1999) and Pfaff (1999) were also used to help develop the survey. The survey contained detailed questions on community characteristics including land-use behaviour. Similar to the survey used in East Kalimantan, this one had a closed format thus leaving little room for interpretation and allowing for a direct, cross-community comparison. Data on land-use collected in the communities are to be compared with GIS data collected in 2007.

This survey was under severe time constraints hence necessitating the selection and training of a large research team to ensure that data collection was completed by August 2006. Thus, 12 enumerators along with one re-search assistant joined the research team for a two month fieldwork period. Training and the survey pre-test took place over a two week period at the end of May 2006. Time constraints also meant that the original 2001 community sample had to be reduced from 80 to 72. Moreover, we had to drop the idea of incorporating a household survey as a means of corroborating the com-munity-level findings, similar to my studies in East Kalimantan. Each com-munity was visited for four days and again, the field team were encouraged to ask questions around the format of the survey in order to build a picture of the situation in each community. This enabled us to gather information that may not be captured using the formal survey, which is complemented by the large amount of qualitative information already contained within Mappatoba (2004) and Birner and Mappatoba (2002). Despite the relative speed with which this survey had to be completed, both the quantitative and qualitative survey data are of reasonably high quality, which were confirmed with com-parisons with data from the 2001 survey in addition to the findings from previous studies.

## 4. Discussion

In each of the four Indonesian studies, I combined quantitative and qualita-tive research approaches. Given my disciplinary background, I tend towards a more quantitative approach as a result of my training and its usefulness with respect to obtaining a broader picture of policy impacts and social and envi-ronmental trends outside a local context. I have a degree in biology and two in economics and hence, have long been trained in the 'scientific method' and in using quantitative data and methods of data analysis. For any researcher, how research is undertaken will be conditional on one's background and training. Nevertheless, despite experiencing at first hand the difficulties in for learning and working across disciplines, with patience and a willingness to learn it is possible to gain an understanding of another discipline to the bene-fit of one's research. One way to build on your own research background is to collaborate with people of different backgrounds. For example, while working for CIFOR I worked with a number of anthropologists. In particular on the illegal logging project, I had a particularly fruitful working partnership with one anthropologist. My colleague was able to explain the inter-relations between Indonesian villagers and their forests, and I was able to reciprocate by explaining the economic incentives underlying the networks of corruption fuelling and benefiting from illegal logging. We have continued to cooperate on research and share insights up to the present day.

Collaboration and networking are the lifeblood of undertaking good research but scientists can be very competitive and protective of what they perceive as their 'research territories'. Other anthropological and sociological colleagues at CIFOR, while sceptical of my integrated approach at first, in time became more receptive as they realised that I was incorporating much of their research approaches and findings into my own work. I was also able to show that we had more to gain through collaboration and data sharing than working alone. That said, scientists from different backgrounds tend to develop and use their own jargon, which sometimes obscures even basic ideas. The heavy use of mathematics in economic theory is sometimes a barrier to non-economists wanting to borrow ideas from this discipline. Similarly, the use of detailed narratives by social anthropologists and sociologists sometimes appear incomprehensible for people working outside these disciplines who are maybe looking for more precision. More open and better quality communication, without the use of unnecessary jargon, would help break down the barriers across disciplines.

Despite my background in quantitative data analysis, I am well aware that there are aspects of my research that are not readily amenable to quantification. This became increasingly clear the longer I worked in a particular region or area. For example, power relations among community elites and their relations to local business and government elites certainly influenced some of the outcomes from the logging agreements negotiated after decentralization. In Palmer (2006), a number of chapters are devoted to analysing these kinds of aspects of my research, aspects that could not be directly measured nor analysed quantitatively alone. Combining the data analysis with detailed qualitative information helped to bridge these data gaps. That said, new methods have been and are being developed, which can complement qualitative observations and descriptions. For example, Engel and Palmer (2006) developed an indicator of ethnic heterogeneity, which was used as a factor of collective action ability among communities in East Kalimantan. In another study, I observed the importance of leadership in intra- an inter-community collective active with regards to the enforcement of community property rights over the forest (see Palmer, 2004). In a follow-up paper, I supplemented the information from the aforementioned study with quantitative data in order to separate out the effects of leadership from other impacts on the ability of communities to enforce their property rights (see Palmer, 2007). Statistical methods can be very useful when used to demonstrate whether your variables have any relation to the phenomena under study and show what knowledge is missing; results from my regression analyses showed, for example, that only up to 50 percent of the variation in outcomes could be explained with variables that could be measured in any meaningful way (see Engel and Palmer, 2006).

While pure sociological and anthropological research approaches typically involve spending more time in research areas, using more open-ended questions and relying heavily on participant observation (see for example, Wall, Veldwisch, this volume), the methodology used in this study attempted to blend aspects of these approaches with quantitative data collection into a more rigorous and systematic methodology. The use of an economic conceptual framework to analyse many of the responses from the surveys required that the research was undertaken in this way. Nevertheless, the trade-off was clear: a loss of detail at for each community surveyed and limited opportunity for observation in exchange for a shorter period of time in each of a larger sample of communities.

In my experience, there was a limit to how much useful information could be gathered from the majority of respondents interviewed due to their limited experiences of and participation in the research phenomena under study. From the perspective of my research, this was in itself an interesting result, although it added little to my understanding of the causal relationships underlying the outcomes of interest. These could only be understood at the community level and beyond, e.g. timber prices at the regional level, behaviour of logging firms, etc. The systematic observation of logging practices and the 'accidental discovery' of practices, which were not reported in the survey and interviews, would have been interesting but very time consuming. In particular, where the subject matter is sensitive as in illegal logging, many respondents may not be willing to volunteer too much information anyway and hence, there is an argument for concentrating on 'key informants'. It is important to be aware of selectivity bias in selecting respondents and account for this 'elite-focused bias' in any analysis. Of course, the exact approach taken will be conditional on the nature of the research in hand and for research topics in which a wider variety of observations can be obtained, the optimal research strategy would be to sample as many of these as possible.

Social science as a whole focuses on social and cultural phenomena and increasingly with development studies, on environmental issues too. It is thus necessary to try to understand social-environmental interactions in a broader context, i.e. not just at the level of a household or community. Even where it is possible to focus on the individual level such as in psychological studies, it is impossible to undertake research without due consideration of the broader social and environmental context in which the subject lives. Moreover, psychological studies commonly incorporate 'control groups' and statistical analysis. Social-anthropologists, on the other hand, tend to employ purely qualitative methods compared to the methods employed in other social sciences (see Bernard, 1994). Typically, this type of approach results in a rich seam of qualitative and sometimes, quantitative data too, although in the absence of statistical methods, testing for data quality and reliability is quite a serious problem. Bernard (1986:392) notes that anthropologists need to be aware of these issues and to take the appropriate steps, including exposure to advances in techniques in other disciplines that improve data validity and reliability. Moreover, in moving beyond detailed narratives of the phenomena in hand, there are problems in such an approach alone providing a testable basis for explaining the relationships among the factors underlying this.[2] In the context of environmental and development research, where many factors and actors interact on different scales, it seems unlikely that many of these can be observed within the typical, small-scale research area of many social-anthropological studies. Perhaps more crucially, the counter-factual comparison is not important in social-anthropological research. With regards to policy evaluation and policy-making, this is perhaps the major weakness of using a purely qualitative approach alone. For many policy-makers searching for a deeper understanding of social-economic and environmental interactions on a broader scale, a detailed narrative of a particular case may not provide enough information by which to make and implement policy, and can sometimes lead to policy by 'conventional wisdom' (Levitt and Dubner, 2005). This might explain why policy analysts in development studies tend to prefer to work on the basis of quantitative data and data analysis, although a dependence on this approach is also fraught with problems: numbers are frequently poorly sourced, poorly collected, poorly analysed and poorly understood.

A reliance of quantitative/statistical data alone can lead to problems. Economists, in particular, typically base their analyses on government data. For example, in reviewing economic models used for assessing the causes of deforestation, Angelsen and Kaimowitz (1999) note that a number of analyses utilized forest cover data that were clearly of dubious quality despite originating from the Food and Agriculture Organization's (FAO) Forest Resource Assessments. Self-collected data, particularly below the national level, is a better approach because at least the researcher will be fully aware of the flaws with his or her data and can at least deal with the results in a more pragmatic manner. A researcher with field experience is also in a better position to support the numbers with good quality qualitative observations, which at the minimum can bring the quantitative data 'to life'. Without the qualitative insights and intuition, any kind of statistical analysis can look overly mechanical. For instance, qualitative insights can lend themselves to a deeper understanding of the causal processes underlying phenomena, and help differentiate these from those factors that merely appear to be statistically correlated. Moreover, local-level phenomena can often be over-looked when focusing on statistics alone. With regard to the interpretation of results for policy in the local context, researchers need to be careful in reading too much into the numbers. For example, following an excellent statistical analysis on the causes of land-use changes in Indonesia, Maertens (2004) overlooked the local institutional context when discussing the policy implications of the results. Thus, some of the policy implications suggested were mechanically derived from interpretations of the data without due consideration of context-specific factors on the ground. These factors may, however, have been less amenable to direct measurement. In summary, a combination of quantitative measurements and qualitative, context-specific insights optimise the policy relevance of empirical research in developing countries.

An in-depth understanding and knowledge of one's research subject is essential to support the quantitative data, whether the latter show conclusive results or not. Simply blinding your audience with state-of-the-art statistical methods is not a positive way of imparting and communicating your research findings. But, on the other hand, the direct, qualitative comparison of cases without the use of quantitative data will be subject to the problems of how to obtain objective results and then to present these in an objective a manner as possible. For example, if one was to ask how villagers how they perceive 'poverty' in Indonesia and Bolivia and then directly compare the results, you will have little way of knowing whether poverty is more pronounced in one place or the other. Recently there has been a lot of development in methods in qualitative comparative studies, (see for example, Rihoux, 2006). However, there is still the question of whether or not cases can be compared as objectively as using qualitative data alone. One might argue that a large number of case studies showing similar results can at least prod policy in one direction or another. Nevertheless, the variety of methods used in undertaking these kinds of studies and hence, an inability to directly and reliably compare these still leaves problems for policy making. This may be another reason why policy-makers tend to be more comfortable working with quantitative data than forming policy on the basis of narrative accounts alone. Thus, while this dependence on numbers is perhaps questionable, it is important for researchers in the development research field to be comfortable in working with these and ensure that policy-makers do not misinterpret them.

Knowledge and experience of an area, beyond that gained from secondary research, assists in research preparation and avoiding the pitfalls in undertaking fieldwork in a developing country context. In this respect, 'specialists' have an advantage over 'generalists'. The latter may be more dependent on expert opinions in the interpretation of their data than the former who will have a better-formed intuition on what is happening at the local level. For outsiders to a particular country, building contacts and networks is important for preparing fieldwork. A good knowledge of the local language is key for this as is being sensitive to the local cultural context. Language is also important to actually undertaking research for relying on translators often results in misunderstandings and sometimes the gathering of erroneous data. During all my studies, I undertook fieldwork in the local language and also had research assistants write down the points of discussion, which I could translate in my own time later. While time-consuming, this strategy ensured that I missed relatively little from sometimes fast-moving discussions in the field. People who undertake research in their home countries will not have these problems, although it is important that they remain impartial with respect to their research subjects, something that some of the Indonesians working in my research teams found hard to do at times.

Keeping your research assistants informed and motivated about the goals of your research can help mitigate the impartiality problem as well as ensuring that they work honestly and to the best of their abilities on your behalf. Spending 'quality time' with each, individual assistant in the field worked well for me in East Kalimantan, as it gave people a chance to ask questions about the motivations behind the research and gave me an opportunity to deal with individual problems or issues as they arose. This also helped all of us to get to know one another better and helped maintain individual motivation. It was important that everyone felt like a valued member of the team. Building 'team spirit' certainly helped maintain morale when conditions were difficult and decisions had to be taken for the 'good of the team'. Of course, the quality of local research assistants will depend on many factors but with the right amount of training and survey pre-testing, local people will not only give you an extra insight into local conditions but can prove to be perfectly capable of carrying out most types of survey. For example, I recruited a young, local Indonesian language teacher with no prior field experience who was keen for an opportunity to undertake fieldwork. Despite my initial reservations, she turned out to be my best field assistant in East Kalimantan and has since gone on to work for CIFOR and the Nature Conservancy (TNC), has undertaken a social science M.Sc.in Indonesia and is currently working on her PhD in social-anthropology at Wageningen University in the Netherlands. That said, the selection of assistants is an important process that should not be rushed. In particular, when recruiting people who work for local NGOs, care needs to be taken to ensure that they do not bring their 'other work' into your research project. During my projects in East Kalimantan, two of my assistants were found to be incorporating their outside work into my survey and were even caught sub-contracting survey work to their family members. In these instances, 'people management' in the local context is important to overall 'project management' and is something that I learnt through trial and error rather than through any formal training.

There are a number of problems with setting up large samples, aside from the usual logistical and financial constraints. First, there may be problems with random sampling on a wide scale where government data are nonexistent or of poor quality. One way around this is to undertake an exploratory fieldtrip to gather some basic information on the ground. During such a trip, one could undertake informal interviews and discussions with key informants along with simple observations. Regardless of method used, the important idea is to get a feel for what the conditions on the ground and to obtain a basic idea of the kinds of questions you might ask in order to address your research objectives. These, of course, would then need to be more formally tried out during survey pre-testing. Second, the sampling of a large number of communities or households requires controlling for a potentially large amount of variation. Within East Kalimantan, many of the communities shared similar characteristics and the framework for logging negotiations was the same from district to district. Building up knowledge and thorough preparation are important in establishing the contours of your field research. Third, for direct comparisons across households or communities, survey questions should be designed in order to minimise the level of interpretation from the research subject, unless of course, the research is about respondents' attitudes and opinions. Furthermore, right from the beginning it is important to ensure that everything in your surveys is clearly defined. A failure to do this, again, leaves room for different interpretations. Finally, once you have your data how do you verify it's accuracy, particularly where government data are poor? In East Kalimantan, I had two differing surveys that interviewed people on two levels within a community and could use these to cross-check and corroborate both my qualitative and quantitative findings. Fortunately, I was also able to cross-check and validate some of my data with previous research. Where this is not possible, researchers should be prepared either to design different surveys for different, defined groups of research subjects or to combine survey methods with completely different methods altogether (see for example, Wall in this volume).

## 5. Conclusions

In conclusion, there are weaknesses in undertaking either a pure qualitative study or quantitative data-driven research alone. While some researchers such as Flyvbjerg (2006) may argue that social science may be strengthened by the execution a greater number of case studies, I would argue that research is better served by a greater number of cases but with an effort made to measure the objects of interest and by putting the data through a statistical workout. At the same time, a great deal of qualitative information can be gathered from key informants to put a human face onto the numbers and provide empirical support to these. In economics, the gathering of qualitative information is not valued as much as it should be and the reliance of statistical analysis alone is a weakness that needs to be addressed in the design of field research on environment and development. By doing so, much economic analysis would not only be enriched but also provides a route of communication with non-economists. Likewise, sociologists and anthropologists would also benefit from incorporating some quantitative data analysis into their research to support their narratives (as many political scientists already do) and as means of reaching out to people outside their own fields. The question then is in deciding the appropriate mix of quantitative and qualitative data collection, which will be dependent on research objectives and on a researcher's training and background. Working directly with researchers from other backgrounds, similar to my experience of working with CIFOR's anthropologists, can also help in the development of new methods where formal training is lacking. Scientists are often, however, very competitive people and while this competition can be healthy, pushing up standards of research, it sometimes makes collaboration harder to achieve. Good communication and an understanding of the gains of collaboration can be a way towards collaboration with scientists from other disciplines. Nevertheless, even a well-funded, cross-disciplinary and integrated study should be aware that not everything that occurs in the field can be observed and that not everything that can be observed, can be interpreted logically. In this sense, we should all heed Hayek's warning about informational problems when we undertake field research (see Hayek, 1945). Undertaking research in developing countries is a more difficult challenge than that in a developed country context but with greater creativity, innovation and the willingness to glance across disciplines on the part of the researcher, policy to reconcile environmental and developmental objectives can only be extended and improved.

## Notes

[1] See Levitt and Dubner (2005) for an informal account of how statistical methods are used to counter the conventional wisdom in a number of policy areas.

[2] For more on the debate on 'cause and effect' in anthropology, see O'Meara (1997).

## References

Agrawal, A., and J. Ribot (1999) 'Accountability in decentralization: a framework for South Asian and African cases.' *Journal of Developing Areas* 33:473-502

André, C. and J. Platteau (1998) 'Land relations under unbearable stress: Rwanda caught in the Malthusian trap.' *Journal of Economic Behaviour and Organization* 34(3):1–47

Angelsen, A., and D. Kaimowitz (1999) 'Rethinking the causes of deforestation: Lessons from economic models.' *The World Bank Research Observer* 14(1):73-98

Baland, J. M., and J. P. Platteau (1996) *Halting degradation of natural resources. Is there a role for rural communities?*: Food and Agriculture Organization of the United Nations (FAO) and Clarendon Press, Rome, Italy and Oxford, UK

Barr, C., E. Wollenberg, G. Limberg, N. Anau, R. Iwan, M. Sudana, M. Moeliono, and Djogo, T. (2001) The impacts of decentralization on forests and forest-dependent communities in Malinau district, East Kalimantan. *Decentralization and forests in Indonesia series: case study 3.*, Center for International Forestry Research (CIFOR), Bogor

Bernard, H. R. (1994) *Research methods in cultural anthropology.* second edition, Sage, Thousand Oaks CA

Bernard, H. R., Pelto, P. P., Werner, O., Boster, J., Romney, A. K., Johnson, A., Ember, C. R., and A. Kasakoff (1986) 'The construction of primary data in anthropology.' *Cultural Anthropology* 27(4):382-396

Birner, R., and M. Mappatoba (2002) 'Community-based agreements on conservation in Central Sulawesi – A coase solution to externalities or a case of empowered deliberative democracy?' *STORMA Discussion Paper Series on Social and Economic Dynamics in Rainforest Margins* 3, Göttingen and Bogor

Boos, M. (1992) *A typology of case studies.* Rainer Hampp Verlag, München and Mering

Bryman, A. (2006) 'Integrating quantitative and qualitative research: how is it done?' *Qualitative Research* 6(1):97-113

Callister, D. J. (1999) 'Corrupt and illegal activities in the forestry sector: current understandings and implications for World Bank forest policy.' Paper prepared for the *Forest Policy Implementation Review and Strategy Development: Analytical Studies.* World Bank Group, Washington DC

Casson, A., and K. Obidzinski (2002) 'From New Order to regional autonomy: shifting dynamics of 'illegal' logging in Kalimantan, Indonesia.' *World Development* 30(12):2133–2151

Engel, S., R. López, and C. Palmer (2006) 'Community-industry contracting over natural resource use in a context of weak property rights: the case of Indonesia.' *Environmental and Resource Economics* 33(1):73-93

Engel, S, and C. Palmer (2006) 'Who owns the right? The determinants of community benefits from logging in Indonesia.' *Forest Policy and Economics* 8(4): 434-446

Engel, S., and R. López (2004) 'Exploiting common resources with capital-intensive technologies: the role of external forces.' *ZEF Discussion Papers on Development Policy* 90. Center for Development Research, University of Bonn

Ethridge, D. (2004) *Research methodology in applied economics*. Blackwell, Oxford

Ferraro, P. J., and S. K. Pattanayak. (2006) 'Money for nothing? A call for empirical evaluation of biodiversity conservation easements.' *PLoS Biology* 4(4):1-6

Flyvbjerg, B. (2006) 'Five misunderstandings about case-study research.' *Qualitative Inquiry* 12(2):219-245

Hayek, F. (1945) 'The use of knowledge in society.' *American Economic Review* 35(4): 519-30

Larson, A. M., and J. Ribot (2004) 'Democratic decentralization through a natural resource lens: an introduction.' *European Journal of Development Research* 16(1):1-25

Levitt, S. D., and S. J. Dubner (2005) *Freakanomics. A rogue economist explores the hidden side of everthing*. Penguin, London

López, R.. (1998) 'Where development can or cannot go: the role of poverty-environment linkages.' In: B. Pleskovic and J. Stiglitz (eds.) *Annual Bank Conference on Development Economics 1997*. The World Bank Press, Washington, DC

Maertens, M. (2004) *Economic modelling of land-use patterns in forest frontier areas. Theory, empirical assessment and policy implications for Central Sulawesi, Indonesia*. Dissertation.de-Verlag, Berlin

Mappatoba, M. (2004) *Co-management of protected areas: the case of community agreements on conservation in the Lore Lindu National Park, Central Sulawesi, Indonesia*. Dissertation, Cuvillier Verlag, Göttingen

McCarthy, J.F. (2000) *Wild logging: the rise and fall of logging networks and biodiversity conservation projects on Sumatra's rainforest frontier*. CIFOR Occasional Paper 31, Center for International Forestry Research (CIFOR), Bogor

O'Meara, T. (1997) Causation and the struggle for the science of culture. *Current Anthropology* 38(3): 399-418

Onwuegbuzie, A., and N. Leech (2005) 'On becoming a pragmatic researcher: the importance of combining quantitative and qualitative research methodologies.' *International Journal of Social Science Methodology: Theory and Practice* 8(5):375-387

Palmer, C., and S. Engel (2007) 'For better or for worse? Local impacts of the decentralization of Indonesia's forest sector.' forthcoming in *World Development* end-2007

Palmer, C. (2007) 'The role of leadership in the collective enforcement of community property rights in Indonesia.' *Society and Natural Resources* 20(5):397-413

Palmer, C. (2006) The outcomes and their determinants from community-company contracting over forest use in post-decentralization Indonesia. *Development Economics and Policy* 52, Peter Lang, Frankfurt

Palmer, C. (2004) *The role of collective action in determining the benefits from IPPK logging concessions: a case study from Sekatak, East Kalimantan.* Working Paper 28, Center for International Forestry Research (CIFOR), Bogor

Palmer, C. (2001) *The extent and causes of illegal logging: an analysis of a major cause of tropical deforestation in Indonesia.* Working Paper. University College London, The Centre for Social and Economic Research on the Global Environment (CSERGE), London

Ostrom, E. (1990) *Governing the commons: the evolution of institutions for collective action.* Cambridge University Press, Cambridge

Pfaff, A. S. P. (1999) 'What drives deforestation in the Brazilian Amazon? Evidence from satellite and socioeconomic data.' *Journal of Environmental Economics and Management* 37:26-43

Ravallion, M. (2001) 'The mystery of the vanishing benefits: An introduction to impact evaluation.' *The World Bank Economic Review* 15(1):115-140

Resosudarmo, I.A.P. (2004) 'Closer to people and trees: will decentralization work for the people and the forests of Indonesia?' *European Journal of Development Research* 16(1):110-132

Rihoux, B. (2006) 'Qualitative comparative analysis (QCA) and related systematic comparative methods: Recent advances and remaining challenges for social science research.' *International Sociology* 21(5): 679-706

Sánchez-Azofeifa G. A., Daily, G. C., Pfaff, A. S. P. and C. Busch (2003) 'Integrity and isolation of Costa Rica's national parks and biological reserves: Examining the dynamics of land-cover change.' *Biological Conservation* 109:123–135

Scholz, R. W., and O. Tietje (2002) *Embedded case study methods. Integrating quantitative and qualitative knowledge.* Sage Publications, Thousand Oaks, CA

Scotland, N., Fraser, A., and N. Jewell (1999) *Roundwood supply and demand in the forest sector in Indonesia.* Indonesia Tropical Forestry Management Programme (ITFMP) report no. PFM/EC/99/08. Jakarta

Telepak Indonesia and the Environmental Investigation Agency (EIA) (1999) *The final cut: illegal logging in Indonesia's Orangutan parks.* Bogor

Zeller, M., S. Schwarz., and T. van Rheenen (2002) 'Statistical sampling frame and methods used for the selection of villages and households in the scope of the research program on Stability of Rainforest Margins in Indonesia (STORMA).' *STORMA Discussion Paper Series on Social and Economic Dynamics in Rainforest Margins* 1, Göttingen and Bogor

# 6

# Knowledge Resources (Yet) Untapped

## The challenge of finding one's place in an interdisciplinary water research project on the Volta River basin, West Africa.

Irit Eguavoen

## 1. Introduction

Household water serves as an umbrella term to describe what is variously called drinking water, domestic water or potable water. However, it embodies much more than that. People in countries with low drinking water supply coverage also draw water from non-potable sources for primary and productive uses that are performed on household level. The amounts withdrawn from ground and surface water for such uses within the West African Volta River Basin are comparatively small. Therefore, household water uses do not compete with water uses of the other sectors, which consume much larger water quantities. As in most countries, household water in Ghana is excluded from the issuing of administrative water rights or water licences by the national water planning authority (the Ghanaian Water Resources Commission). Despite the rather marginal importance of household water for basin wide water allocation planning, it is of crucial importance for people living within the basin. It is the largest water use in terms of users (100 % of the inhabitants of the Volta Basin) and in terms of number of withdrawals (uncountable on a daily basis). Moreover, it serves a great variety of uses.

That is why the successful integration of interdisciplinary findings on household water has the potential to be a very valuable component of the decision-support system (DSS). This is a computer–based customer's interface that is presently being developed by the GLOWA Volta research project (GVP) to support political decision-making concerning Water Resources Management in Ghana and Burkina Faso. The research project aims to gain an understanding of the complex geo-hydrological and socio-political factors and their interrelations that determine the hydrological cycle within the river basin as well as the changes they undergo due to climate change.[1] For this, a research period of nine years is funded by the BMBF (the German Ministry of Education and Research), which splits into three project phases (2000-2009). During the second project phase, which lasted from June 2003 to May 2006, a number of about one hundred researchers from different natural and social sciences worked in various research institutions in Germany, the Netherlands, Ghana and Burkina Faso to create a sound data base and the decision support system concerning nationwide water allocation, reforms of the institutional and legal framework, as well as development strategies, which relate to water uses, as for example, the introduction of groundwater irrigation in Northern Ghana. Additionally, project alumni are affiliated to other research institutions all over the world. The more the project proceeds in its project cycle, the more important the social and research network with Ghanaian and Burkinabe stakeholders becomes, which further enhances the complexity of the GLOWA Volta project.

When I started my work about four years ago, I gained the impression that research on household water was a rather marginal aspect of the project. Seeing it from today's perspective, I know that I was somehow wrong because by this point in time, I was neither familiar enough with the first and second project proposals nor did I have a good overview on the overall project, on the participants as well as on their current occupation. When I wrote my individual research proposal, I integrated existing project documentation and publications, and talked to colleagues; but despite this I was not fully aware what research on household water currently took place. This was due to a number of factors, such as the size and complexity of the project, the short time period of three months for proposal writing, the unfinished stage of other PhD and publication projects, as well as the absence of colleagues who conducted research in Ghana and Burkina Faso by this point in time. The first phase GLOWA Volta completion report that could have helped me to detect my exact place and task in the project and to link my own research more to what was done in the previous project phase was published when I was already busy conducting my field research in Ghana (ZEF/ GVP, 2005a).[2]

Very much to my own surprise, my work on local household water management turned out to be a rather lonely business despite the fact that other work was conducted on household water during the same period. When this chapter was prepared, there was no forum for knowledge exchange on household water but instead a large number of scattered research results, publications and people – most of us unaware of what the other person was exactly doing. No person was engaged or appointed by the project to oversee all research done on household water and to integrate the results or to lead the discussion among the respective researchers.

The GLOWA Volta research project is now in its third and last project phase. This is the time to integrate knowledge and to wrap up results. Whilst this task seems to work out well in other parts of the project, which are considered as most crucial for the DSS, such as irrigation and climate change, I don't experience this for the household water component. But in my opinion, the neglect of existing data and results in the period of interdisciplinary knowledge integration may result in a situation in which a part of the gained knowledge run the risk to go down the drain; meaning that its potential will be not fully tapped. This chapter argues that interdisciplinary research in complex projects is in practice a manifestation of both, the chance to generate innovative knowledge and at the same time a serious constraint for data integration, processes requiring not only openness and curiosity, but also much personal commitment. Moreover, it illustrates that the way a project is planned and organized has an impact on the degree of subsequent collaboration among its researchers, as well as on the efficiency to generate innovative research results.

Writing this chapter was driven by personal curiosity and interest as well as the need for a knowledge inventory on project level and an analysis of the factors, which had contributed to poor extent of interdisciplinary collaboration within a particular project cluster so far. It was thought to serve as impulse for change and improvement. Even though it is a rather personal account, the chapter intends to elaborate on two general issues.

1. How was interdisciplinary research on household water conceptualized in the three project proposals?

2. How does interdisciplinary knowledge exchange and sharing take place in practice, and how can and should knowledge resources be better tapped within the project?

The following section shows how household water in the project was conceptualized theoretically and what research was planned to be conducted on it. The review of the proposals already hints at some structural reasons for the low visibility of household water within the project and the rather little collaboration among researchers. Section three tells about the data collection and data base on household water. It further looks at intra-project collaboration between researchers from different disciplines in practice. The article ends with a discussion of problems in interdisciplinary research collaboration and an outlook to current and future work in section four.

## 2. Conceptualizing interdisciplinary research - Setting the course for practical collaboration

### *Incentives for interdisciplinary collaboration*

Research on household water faces the same challenge as research on any other natural resource subject does. Its complexity requires knowledge and understanding that frequently exceeds disciplinary boundaries and professional capacities of individual researchers. Therefore, research on natural resources is mainly conducted by researchers and research projects committed to disciplinary hybrids and sub-disciplines. New Institutional Economics, Ecological Anthropology, Environmental History or Political Ecology provide such examples of the on-going and probably never-ending search for more integrative ways to gain meaningful insight on natural resources. Methodologies and theories from different disciplinary origins get linked up to generate innovative scientific knowledge. Data sets usually include quantitative natural science data of different scales but also quantitative and qualitative social science, as well as historical data. Returning to household water, a number of research areas can be identified, which partly intersect or stand in theoretical and practical co-relation to each other and suggest an interdisciplinary approach to investigate the subject. Geology, Hydrology, Meteorology, Ecology and Medicine form the natural science components. Anthropology, Political Science, Economics and History being social and humanistic sciences are also components of the endeavour. Geography contributes to both components depending on its practice as Physical or Social Geography.

As illustrated in figure 6.1 below, the research topic of 'household water', as I approached it in my field study, touched several disciplinary boundaries. The ethnographic research design aimed at a holistic approach, which could capture the role of water for the local livelihood, its local meaning, as well as the ways water supply was locally organized and embedded into a legal system in past and present time.

**Figure 6.1 A holistic approach to household water**

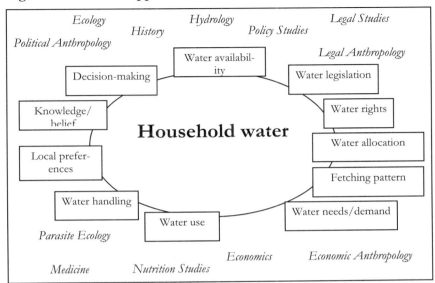

Any less holistic approach would have focused on one or two of such boundary areas and deepened its understanding by following up a specific data collection and analytical method – for the price of losing the general view on the subject. Whilst the advantage of a holistic approach is to cover the subject as widely as possible and to show linkages between areas of research, its disadvantage lies in the superficiality, which eventually occurs in the boundary areas. The latter makes the single researcher vulnerable for critique coming from the other disciplinary side of the boundary area as well as from his disciplinary colleagues. However, social anthropologists enjoy the doubtful and sometimes nasty reputation of "knowing a little about everything (but nothing in particular)" but they usually don't mind because they know about the strength of their integrative approach. Ideally, researchers in interdisciplinary projects may bridge and investigate such superficial boundary areas by exchange of their ideas, data and expertise. The absolute pre-condition for that is the contact of these researchers, be it personal, via means of communication and/or via the acknowledgement of each others written work.

## Planning interdisciplinary research

The terminology 'household water' is not found in the project proposals; it is conceptualised as both communal and household supply (including non-potable water sources) or as drinking water (excluding non-potable water sources). The first and second proposals contain a research cluster that is focused on household water under the heading "Water Use" (W-subproject). This title is already prone to lead to confusion because the sub-projects in the first proposal, which were categorized under "Water Use", included (W-1) Run-off and hydraulic routing, (W-2) Integrated economic and hydrologic optimisation, (W-3) Health and water, (W-4) Communal and household water supply and (W-5) Institutional Analysis. The sub-project also included water use for hydropower under W-3 (ZEF/GVP, 1999).

A review of the first project proposal shows that the sub-projects W-1 and W-2 related to household water insofar as they give hydrological insight on the resource availability. The W-3 water and health subproject only addressed malaria, although other significant diseases were identified in the Volta Basin. The research question "What is the distribution of malaria, its vectors and access to health services and how are they related to surface, irrigation and drinking water?" was posed in the proposal (ibid.: 36-37). For household water research, other diseases, such as water-washed diarrhoeal diseases or water-born diseases, such as guinea worm, would have been of larger interest because in contrast to these diseases, there is no direct relationship between malaria and improved water provision but only indirect ones, which concerns e.g. environmental sanitation (the avoidance of standing water that could serve as vector for the mosquitoes).

The part of the first proposal that explains subproject W-4 was mainly based on an overview article by Webb and the project participant Iskandarani (1998), who identified the research needs in the Volta basin. The derived research questions are very basic for the investigation of local household water situations. The whole sub-project was conceptualised as a pure domain of statistics and econometrics:

> "The major objective of the study is to assess water security at the community and household level [...] The assessment of drinking water demand will be an essential input into the economic optimisation model and will also be informed by the outcomes of the hydraulic modelling. The household water demand analysis will: (1) serve as a demand and cost variable for the integrated economic-hydrological-institutional water allocation model; (2) provide a planning basis and tool for future adequate demand responsive household water supply." "The analysis will basically fol-

low two complementary approaches: (1) Econometric analysis of the determinants of water demand and water price (2) Development of a community and household model for maximising utility of water    consumption    for domestic and agricultural use with time and water access    as    constraints." (ZEF/GVP, 1999: 65).

Sub-project W-5 was conceptualized to gain knowledge on national, regional, local and transboundary WRM institutions. It considered of interest how efficient they were working and how they were embedded into power relations. An in depth stakeholder analysis was planned, as well as an overview over "actual international co-ordination efforts". Incentives and obstacles for international co-operation should be identified (ibid.: 67-68). Other intended areas of research were local institutions (especially community-based WRM) and local water allocation systems as well as the relationship between riparian parties.

> "The subproject will serve furthermore data collection for the subproject W-2: "Integrated economic-hydrologic optimization" It will give subproject W-4: "Communal and household water use" realistic parameters with a view to the allocation of water resources on different economic sectors, integrating the relative power and influence of the different interest groups on the respective government agencies." (ibid.: 68).

Although no discussion was made on how to allocate the sub-projects to disciplines, W-1 demanded hydrologists, W-4 automatically required economists whilst W-5 carried the implication of employing anthropologists, sociologists and political scientists. This spectrum reflects also the interdisciplinary composition of the proposal writing team, emphasizing the importance of project design for disciplinary collaboration. Despite such heterogeneous team, it seems that the proposal writing was dominated by practitioner of natural sciences and models. Moreover, a hierarchy of significance between the sub-projects was already established by determining their relations and data exchange patterns. For example, the anthropological W-5 sub-project was conceptualized as provider of variables for other sub-projects and general background data. The duty to provide empirical input was determined but the format of that contribution was not. This way, a data divide was created on project level. Instead of tackling the questions of data integration in sub-projects, the question of how to integrate data of different format was postponed to a later point in time and to the overall project level.

The structure of the proposal changed when entering the second project phase. The five sub-projects were summarized into three sub-projects, called

(W-1) Run-off and Hydraulic Routing, (W-2) Water and Livelihood and (W-3) Institutional Analysis (ZEF/GVP, 2002). Here, the separation of disciplines and approaches as created in the documents becomes more obvious. W-1 remained a purely hydrological sub-project; whilst it is not only the data collection and evaluation method but also the rather strict differentiation of tasks between W-2 and W-3, which is striking.

**Figure 6.2 Task sharing in the project (phase I and phase II)**

| W-3 Health and water + W-4 Communal household water supply | W-5 Institutional analysis |
| --- | --- |
| = W-2 Water and livelihood | = W-3 Institutional analysis |
| GVP phase I | |

| | |
| --- | --- |
| • malaria prevalence | • local, regional, national, international institutions for WRM |
| • water demand and usage | |
| • water prices | • power relations |
| • beneficiaries of improved water access | • stakeholder analysis |
| | • local water allocation systems |
| • community participation | • relationship between riparian countries |
| • knowledge transfer | |
| • behaviour change | |

| GVP phase II | |
| --- | --- |
| • household water demand | • polices and implementation |
| • household water usage | • actors, interest groups, decision-making and negotiation processes |
| • health status, malaria risk map | |
| • water quality | • processes of communication |
| | • institutions of water management |
| | • regulation of privatization |

In the second proposal, the domestic water use cluster of the W-2 economics subproject was conceptualized in a way, which considers economic, political, hydrological and institutional aspects. It moreover dealt with qualitative and quantitative data sets. It seems that there was no institutional link created to the anthropological/sociological W-3 sub-project, which was concerned with similar questions but approached them with a different methodology and theory.

In the third proposal, the former structure of the sub-projects was then completely dissolved and made place for four new methodologically-oriented sub-projects which currently integrate research results and prepare knowledge transfer to Ghanaian and Burkinabe stakeholders. The short descriptions of the current sub-projects presented on the project homepage give an unclear idea of what will be done with collected data on household water. The proposal for sub-project D-1 states "The nucleus of the [decision support system] is the water optimization model, which represents the decision rules and constraints of water users..." Here all water users and water uses are referred to, assumingly also users of household water. The sub-project D-2 rather seems to neglect household water because it

"... models to understand and predict the likely responses of households to environmental and policy changes [...] and the identification of causal factors underlying the household's [...] water use decisions. We will concentrate on the adoption of irrigation practices and on household migration habits..." (GVP homepage).

Household water, which still enjoyed some importance during the second project period, seems to have fallen out of the endeavour of overall data integration in phase three. Interestingly, the complete proposal presents a very different idea.

"The priority tasks related to domestic water demand during Phase III are (i) the estimation of per capita water demand, and the factors underlying demand (e.g. income) for urban households, and (ii) spatial extrapolation and aggregation of domestic water demand both in rural and urban areas in accordance with spatial units defined by the structure and coverage of the node link network of the integrated basin model. Cost–benefit analysis of improved water sources will be required." (ZEF/GVP, 2005b: 59).

The data, to feed the models and calculations were planned to be drawn from the CSF-survey data set.

To summarize, the project proposals are clearly informed by the paradigm of Integrated Water Resources Management. This is reflected in the overall complex structure of the project, which ranges from the subject of hydrology to issues like livelihood, migration, institutions, ecology and embodies almost the full spectrum of disciplines. Exactly the same can also be recognized for the subject of household water. Here, although perhaps parasite ecology and studies of nutrition would have also been of interest, the most important aspects of the subject were seriously considered in the planning process. Hence, the good motivation for interdisciplinary work among the researchers who collaborated during the proposal writing process are clearly translated to the document. But the proposal also indicates the need for interdisciplinary working experience, which in this particular case not all authors had yet because many of them had just started their professional career.

Somehow, in the course of the on-going project, the interest in the institutional set up of household water management, as well as in other qualitative research areas was lost on project level. Under the need to deliver operational models for the Decision Support System, the orientation and attention shifted to strictly quantitative questions: water use schedules, willingness to pay study, minimum acceptable level of consumption, value of access to improved water etc. In practice, qualitative questions of household water continued to be addressed in phase three research among members of W-3 without being stressed or visible in the third project proposal.

It is striking how the proposals already set the course for future research by not only defining the subject and target of overall research as well as the research components but also setting up an organizational framework. It automatically – even though not intentionally – contributed to the segregation of disciplines, leading to a low level of cross cutting cooperation in the beginning of the research project and a hierarchy of significance of single research components. The project was built up in a way so that it did not automatically provide horizontal structures, which connect researchers from different disciplines and of the same thematic subject with each other. Such a forum could have led to early contact and discussion of methodologies, intersectional research interest and compatible data formats.

So, how relevant are such proposals for an individual researcher? In my particular case, the research agenda means that the definition of what belongs to my subject and what does not, was determined by the project proposal and intra-project discussions before going to the field as well as by the expectations of my external supervisor and of the faculty where I planned to submit my dissertation. To stick simply to institutions, regulations and negotiations as suggested in the second research proposal was not possible (compare figure 6.2). Not investigating their social, political and historical dimension and practical impact for water need, use and allocation, as well as for the local livelihood would have disqualified me to gain a degree of my discipline.[3] Even though, digging into linguistics, describing rituals with water and giving a detailed overview on local power relations and old-fashioned custodians of rain is of no (or very little) value for the overall project goal and the Decision Support System, as I fully admit, it had to be done. And I enjoyed doing it because that is what I have studied; this is what I like to do; this is what I can do best and this is the approach I think makes sense to answer my research questions. I guess, this "home feeling" I share with my colleagues, even though we are all affiliated to different disciplinary homes.

## 3. Interdisciplinary collaboration in practice - the lack of intersection

### *The common project data pool – basin wide survey data*

Questions related to household water supply and health formed a substantial part of a basin-wide household survey, which was conducted by the project in two phases (2001). A common sampling frame (CSF) included 501 house-holds living in 20 communities all over the Ghanaian part of the Volta Basin and was later also extended to Burkina Faso. The particular section of the questionnaire aimed at the investigation of data on household water man-agement, access to the resource, consumption, the usage and storage of water within the households, water related expenditures and user's perception of water quality. The latter was then confronted with data on water–related dis-eases, which was colleted in the same survey (Iskandarani et al., 2002).

> "The need for the researchers to undertake their separate enumeration in the same communities was avoided. Thus, interdisciplinary team work by re-searchers is enhanced. In addition, the per capita cost of training enumera-tors or field assistants was reduced by avoiding multiple training sessions" (Osei-Asare, 2005: 28).

An anthropologist from the institutional sub-project worked as coordinator of the enumerators. The large database served several PhD projects, including one on household water security and water demand in the basin (Osei-Asare, 2005) and a comparatively small number of publications on household water (Asante et al., 2002; Engel et al., 2003; Engel et al. forthcoming; Osei-Asare, 2005).

When I developed and later presented my research proposal, I expected the project to communicate what data was needed. Of course, my research design was informed by personal interest and qualification, by the ideas of my supervisor as well as by standards of my own discipline. But I waited for additional guidelines on the format of data, which was required for the modelling or the communication of interest in the elaboration of specific variables. Not receiving them led to some confusion in proposal creation and the first months of writing –up. The discussions with my non-project supervisor pointed out that I felt caught between two stools – writing an individual dissertation and being part of a research project. It was not yet clear, how the project would make use of my contribution. My impression in the middle of the writing-up process was that my research has been written off because it was not conducted within a CSF-community. The decision to drop out from the CSF took place on the level of sub-project coordination and I was never urged to conduct my study in one of the CSF communities.

### Individual data collection – Local field studies

Additional field research was conducted on particular aspects, which deepened the understanding of results from the CSF-survey. Despite the existence of extensive survey data, a geographer conducted an additional household survey on the relationship of water handling practices and the occurrence of diarrhoeal diseases. Her sample derives from the CSF communities. Her focused questionnaire contained 20 questions, which were complemented with water quality sampling and field observations.[4] The CSF-data base was neither used for the generation of findings nor discussed in comparison with results from the project survey, which collected a large amount of data on health and hygiene. It was an economist, who evaluated and analysed that share of data. He hints at the existence of an additional survey but does not refer to the geographer's work though he supported her practically conducting her field survey because her Diploma thesis (written in German) was completed when he (not being able to read German anyway) had already submitted his dissertation. Obviously, no quotable preliminary results were made available for the other colleague beforehand.

Studies on policies and management institutions made no direct use of the available survey data set but only reviewed the results, which were generated by the W-2 colleagues. The field research sites were not within the set of CSF-communities. From the perspective of an economist, the CSF procedure "may lead another potential demerit where other research groups may be unwilling to contribute to this procedure because the likelihood of this random selection missing their sites of interest. This was particularly exemplified in the institutional subgroup which looks for specific issues to study" (Osei-Asare, 2005: 29).

The reasons were threefold. First, it is true that special research interest resulted in site selection outside the CSF-communities. Obviously, as my intention was to observe and collect data about an on-going small town water project, I went, of course, where such a project took place. The other reasons were less obvious.

The second reason for the neglect of the CSF communities was that the survey did not include questions that were of central interest to the sociologists and social anthropologists. Or the questions were formulated in a manner that resulted in responses which were unsatisfying from their disciplinary perspective. I personally doubt, for example, the possibility to gain valid data by asking for example "How often and how many litres of water did you get last month and during a typical month in dry and raining season from the private water vendor and what did you pay per unit?" (Iskandarani et al., 2002) I think, such a question is too confusing for the respondents, too difficult to translate (one risks the translators to create a non-standardized set of sub-questions) as well as it encourages unreliable estimates by the respondents. Researchers from the institutional cluster were asked for a review of the questionnaire but their suggestions were almost ignored. And, of course, I (as any other researcher) will not base my argument on data I don't fully trust. Other questions, of course, were nicely formulated and could have added to my argumentation.

Third, the raw data set was difficult to access and to work with due to ongoing data cleaning but also due to the lack of capacity of the researchers in statistical data analysis. I reviewed existing published results from the econometric calculations but these calculations served a particular research interest of the processing colleague, who had to follow a strict time schedule for his/ her PhD project. Additional results that would have been of interest for me or other project members could not be produced because there was not sufficient staff that could have supported the PhD students, who were not familiar with statistical methods. My time schedule did not allow a training course in SPSS to the level which would have enabled me to work efficiently with the CSF-data. Consequently, results from econometric studies and ethnographic observations hardly show intersection or a common base for discussion.

When I shared the project house with a geo-hydrologist in the beginning of my field stay, she helped me to find an appropriate research site. My later field site is located in exactly the sub-catchment of the Volta River, where she conducted her study on groundwater recharge. My research benefited from this intersection, because household water supply in the village mainly relied on groundwater. This way, the project can subsequently display two inter-linked studies: geo-hydrological and institutional aspects of groundwater for household use. This was an outcome of personal communication and coincident, rather than of planning on project level. It helped to locate myself in the project – outside a CSF-community, what I also communicate during presentations to link myself somehow to the project. Later, the catchment was chosen as pilot for more intense studies. And only due to individual initiative, a joint publication (including an anthropologist and a hydrologist working on groundwater issues in Burkina Faso) is in preparation.

My long-term field study at village level included two surveys. One addressed local water committees. It contained 65 questions; none of which overlaps with the CSF questionnaire. This is because my research interest consisted in the practical performance of local water management and its legal framework. Despite the fact that the results were quantified, there is little chance that they will contribute to the modelling exercises. The second survey addressed more than 100 compounds. Also here, my research interest was a particular one, mainly the gain of orientation knowledge in preparation of the interviews and observations. The questionnaire and sample selection served a special research purpose and are not compatible with the CSF-data because why collect data which was neither requested by the project nor of my personal interest? Why to adapt to a standard format, which is more difficult for me to process?

The compatibility of my quantitative data to the modelling exercises is also limited. The qualitative and quantitative data I do have on payment schemes cannot be included even though my data hints at interesting variables. I am not able to quantify under which conditions people decide to pursue additional livelihood activities, but I am able to list these conditions and to stress on the importance of water as resource input for micro-enterprises. Thus, I think that my contribution to the project is to point out relevant variables but not to provide the detailed data sets. This means in fact, that I cannot provide the format of data, which is required to integrate my information in the modelling exercise. This leads to situations, in which I present my results in front of an interdisciplinary audience, some of which do not acknowledge my findings but instead point out what data set they think I should have collected to be able to make statistically relevant statements.

Interestingly, after realizing that part of my work was on water uses and water demand (which was in fact not intended by the project proposal) I met with a lot of interest from project colleagues, who asked me to deliver quantitative data on water demand, which I did not collect because it was of no relevance for my research question. I was sure that the socio-economic sub-project had already produced such numbers. A hydrologist working on groundwater withdrawal in Burkina Faso could inform the project on withdrawal rates from hand pumps; but his unit of analysis was the pumps. Consequently, he had designed his research to measure withdrawal without regard to the subsequent water users. The lack of reliable data on water demand turned out to be one constraint to modelling exercises simply due to such small misunderstandings and lack of communication within the project. I have to admit that although interacting with the hydrologist on a regular basis, I did not know that he measured withdrawal rates from hand pumps until I was writing this paper, when he presented his research results at a GLOWA Volta strategy meeting.

## Interdisciplinary data integration and knowledge generation

The list of possible constraints to implement and make interdisciplinary work is long (e.g. Mc Neill, 1999; Mollinga, 2006; Fuest, 2006). I don't think the main problem within the GLOWA Volta project is a lack of individual commitment to disciplinary collaboration. Nor is it insurmountable differences of disciplinary cultures (for a list of such stereotypes see Fuest 2006). Of course, an ecologist and soil scientist as the project director may "love to see an anthropologist, who is not afraid of numbers" and be more willing to pursue co-authorship (as was eventually done in the project), as well as an anthropologist like myself would be happy to see colleagues from the natural sciences and economy to reflect more the socio-cultural and historical context of their work and be more trustful our quantitative data. But my personal experience is not shaped by confrontation – though conflicts were not absent within the project - but rather by a lack of intersection on academic level, which is caused by organizational weakness of the project. There is little time to sit with colleagues and develop interdisciplinary questions, which are below the overall project goal; co-writership of articles usually takes more time and organizational effort than writing alone – just to name some constraints.

Interdisciplinary cooperation in practice included reading, observing and discussing other people's work (e.g. joining somebody one day to his trip to collect samples), practical and logistical help in the field (e.g. continuing monitoring and paying of an assistant when the colleague had left) as well as the exchange of charts and maps or the possibility to ask questions of under-standing, such as "What does this hydrological abbreviation mean exactly?" Strictly taken, this is not interdisciplinary work. When I approached people, they were always open-minded, interested and helpful. But the project failed in systematically enhancing contact and creating an organizational set-up, which obliged participants to deal with other disciplines in form of joint pro-jects or publications. But I also observed that other research subjects, such as irrigation, enjoy more collaboration among the researchers, more attention within the project – perhaps because they are more obviously in need for geo-hydrological/ meteorological/ socio-economic data integration.

The generation of scientific knowledge that may serve Ghanaian and Burkinabe decision makers is only one pillar of the GLOWA Volta project. The second pillar is to build up local expertise by training African graduates during their PhD research.[5] The Bonn International Graduate School for Development Research at ZEF, which hosts the major part of project re-searchers, faces the challenge of high turn over in personnel. Participants of the doctoral program return to their home countries after graduation or take up other job appointments – and at times also their data sets, their results and their knowledge without leaving a hard copy. Dissertations always evaluate only a part of the collected data. Remaining data sets do not always enjoy later publication because researchers may already be involved in new projects. The early publication of PhD results faces some constraints. The writing up-periods are long; no systematic archive of research documentation and work in progress existed when writing this article. The timeframe of the doctorate program is tight and researchers therefore attend selected disciplinary confer-ences. Moreover, researchers spare less time on co-writing projects and the discussion outside their disciplinary field. The high turn over of personnel at project co-ordination level was identified as additional constraint (Rodgers et al., 2007b).

The progress of the project gets summarized and evaluated in form of annual and status reports. Each of the three years research periods ends with a completion report, the presentation of results and the outline of the next phase. The coordinator of the German project side stated when asked after his management of project participants in a panel discussion on interdisciplinarity "I don't know their business. I make requests on them. I can't manage them due to the different disciplines. The idea is to let them find their way and to pull them to time lines" It is the overall project target which is coordinated and managed. The academic way to the individual contribution is left to the researchers and their academic supervisors, who may be external and unfamiliar with the overall project goal.

A number of findings, which project members generated did not contribute new knowledge on questions of household water but instead tested commonly acknowledged co-relations and applied them to the Volta Basin as well as verified and quantified them for the project area.[6] It was striking, that available work on household water in the Volta basin by scholars, who worked outside the project, was rather unknown or ignored, even when there was a great overlap in research interest. Accessible references were absent in many bibliographies. Furthermore, project colleagues hardly quoted or discussed each other's work. This was less due to the language divide but more caused by structural reasons.

No regular forum for knowledge exchange (e.g. a colloquium) exists, which connects project researchers at ZEF. Individual research proposals, field reports, conference papers and chapter drafts are presented in research groups of the three ZEF departments, which are organized along disciplinary lines and within my ZEF department additionally according to three research subjects; several research projects cross-cut this organisational structure. A colleague used the appropriate image of a three dimensional matrix, in which the doctoral students have to find their way and place to describe the complexity at ZEF. So, this is not a GLOWA Volta intern constrain but one, which is enhanced through the embedment at a large research centre.

The internal project communication is only based on an updated project homepage, one mailing list, and informal face-to face contact as well as regular but rare workshops. Publications of the team members are scattered all over the library. But a literature database serving GLOWA Volta participants was recently established in the ZEF intranet and many publications are also available on the homepage. Ideally, all relevant references, which are found by project members, should be made known or even available to the others. There have been a number of attempts to realize this for particular subprojects. Their sustainability in the long run has been affected by the continuous management of such reference and library system.

Informal exchange of data and information become difficult when face-to-face contacts end. Moreover, the need for an institutionalised data storage and knowledge management was recognized within the project long time ago. The maintenance of a data storage system faced similar constraints as the library. It was difficult to be handled as a side job by a researcher and a person was hired in phase III to dedicate his full working time to the development of a functional data storage and management system.

### *Non-project research*

Academic expertise in the Ghanaian drinking water sector, existed already in the course of the project. But the literature was not integrated into project publications. Water management in Ghana has been subject of research but only one study gained some prominence (Bacho, 2001a). Others were difficult to access because they were conducted as Diploma or Master Theses in Ghana and were not published. The same holds true for some published studies on local household water management, water handling and health aspects, which were neither read nor quoted (e.g. Ampofo, 1997; Akuoko-Asibey, 1994; Kendie, 1992; 1996; 1999; Kendie and Abane, 2001; Mensah, 1998; Hunter, 1997a, 1997b; Bacho, 2001b; Botchway, 2001, 2004; Doe and Khan, 2004) whilst other easier accessible studies with rather low data input were constantly reviewed (e.g. Karikari, 1996; Mensah, 1999). This attitude points out the need for a knowledge inventory exercise, which systematically collects Ghanaian and Burkinabe studies.

Further, the lack of recognition of non-project work is surprising insofar, as the project intends to identify local experts, who can facilitate the knowledge transfer. It hinders the knowledge exchange between research institutions, e.g. between the project and the Loughborough University, which hosts a number of PhD projects about household water in Ghana or the Ghanaian University of Development Studies. Moreover, it misses the chance to locally identify demand in research from an academic perspective. The knowledge on on-going local research is very small because supervisors of Ghanaian and Burkinabe undergraduate students, who work on household water, are not linked to the project.

## 4. Discussion and conclusion

Household water is only one research subject among many others within the GLOWA Volta research project; therefore this personal account only presented a small extract of the GLOWA -Volta project. But a number of typical problems were identified, which occurred also on project level as well as in other complex interdisciplinary research projects. For the high turn-over in scientific personnel seems to be a typical constraint to the continuous work of the project, one could think about strengthening the administrative components in future long-term projects. An efficient and adequate administration unit and the employment of more experts in office administration could serve as the structural back bone of a large research project and tackle data storage, library system, report writing, archival work, as well as the regular organization of events from the first days of such a project. But this requires the possibility to create more such enduring non-scientific positions. This seems to be difficult at current times and requires a re-thinking at the donor's side.

Communication and exchange of ideas across disciplines were enriching and balanced during the first proposal-writing phase. Consequently, the intended interdisciplinary, but factually multi-disciplinary approach is reflected in the project proposal. Due to organizational reasons, this approach did not guide the practical setting up of multi-disciplinary sub-projects. Instead, a hierarchy of significance between the participating disciplines and a future data divide were created in the proposals and enhanced during the project period. The more the project proceeded the larger became the data divide and disciplinary segregation, which has to be bridged in the end of the overall project period to integrate data. The practical cooperation of individual researchers in the field was realized although it does not always reflect in the publications. The most divergent anthropological sub-project stepped out from the CSF-survey and isolated itself this way further. The interdisciplinary approach of the project was dominated by roles and hierarchies introduced by the proposal; researchers conducting institutional research felt in a defensive position (see Fuest, 2006). The project also illustrates that roles and hierarchies may change in the long run under the pressure of final data integration and knowledge transfer to local stakeholders. Interdisciplinary work is not only a matter of proposals and organizational set-ups. Some of the most inspiring articles I reviewed for my dissertation derived from other disciplines (for example, Hunter, 1992, 1997a, 1997b and Destombes, 1999). This indicates that the interdisciplinary challenge is also a matter of personal commitment and individual curiosity.

The optimal or intended level of interdisciplinary work is not reached yet. Because the structure of the project failed in providing an institutional framework for interdisciplinary cooperation, one could assume that cooperation and interdisciplinary knowledge generation would be enhanced if such forum were created. Thematic research groups, such as one for the subject of household water could be established. Communication could be improved by an additional mailing list linking researchers of the same subject. A joint and regularly updated bibliography could be maintained and made accessible to all researchers. Such subject-oriented group would also be the appropriate addressee for questions concerning drinking water policy, which the Decision Support System will be confronted with. Decision-making in Ghana still follows the lines of water sectors despite the paradigm of Integrated Water Resources Management. A Decision Support System, which can provide IWRM insight but also embodies sector-oriented components, would be valuable for local stakeholders.

What other conclusion should be drawn? First of all, household water in Ghana is an exceptionally well documented case, maybe only comparable to the cases of Zimbabwe, Nigeria, South Africa and Tanzania. Moreover, the GLOWA Volta data set will be expanded to Burkina Faso and therefore include transboundary perspectives, a rather innovative field for investigation. The project provided key studies and is of special interest because of the combination of an economic database, the geo-hydrological assessment and in depth studies. So far, the chance to generate innovative research results was missed due to the poor collaboration practice. If interdisciplinary knowledge generation will be pushed further, it will generate a scientific contribution, which exceeds the major target of the project that is policy support. Second, non-project contributions should find more recognition than is presently the case. Third, not creating an effective organizational set-up, which supports researcher's curiosity, and taps existing knowledge resources, would be a pity.

## Notes

[1] The Volta River Basin covers ca. 400.000 km² of mainly Ghanaian and Burkinabe territory but also minor parts of Ivory Coast and Togo. For detailed information see Rodgers et al. (2007a) and the project homepage www.glowa.volta.de

[2] Very generally, project documents written for donors, show some tendency to present projects in a better light and do usually not give a realistic picture of what was exactly done, which results are already available, or which collaboration has really taken place. As such, they should be rather read as historic documents, which follow an intention in a particular context. Being a new member in a project, one cannot but believe in the reports, the structure, the timelines etc. because one has not yet the contextual information for its interpretation. In comparison with the phase I completion report, the projects was more able to discuss internal challenges, difficulties and the way these were tackled in the phase II completion report because the project could already display more research results  and publications. Further, funding of phase III was already on-going and therefore, there was less need to up-hold a perfect image towards the donor (Rodgers et al., 2007b). Glossing over difficulties by this point in time could eventually have been perceived by the donor as cover-up strategy.

[3] A colleague working in another interdisciplinary project at ZEF was confronted with the statement: "Nice, but this is not ethnography" when presenting his field report at the Max-Planck-Institute for Social Anthropology.

[4] None of the questions was the same although they addressed partly the same or similar issues ("Where do you store the water you fetched?" versus "Out of which material is the drinking vessel made?" and giving different options for response).  Responses could therefore not directly be related to each other (Osei-Asare, 2005; Carbone, 2004).

[5] During the second project phase, fifteen doctoral and master students from Ghana and seven students from other African countries completed their theses in the context of the project (Rodgers et al., 2007b).

[6] For an overview on existing knowledge on household water in Africa see e.g. Thompson et al. (2001), Rosen and Vincent (1999).

# References

Akuoko-Asibey, A. (1994) 'Assessing hygiene and health related improvements of a rural water supply and sanitation programme in northern Ghana.' *Natural Resources Forum* 18:49-54

Akuoko-Asibey, A. (1996) 'A summative evaluation of a rural water supply programme in Ghana.' *Applied Geography* 16:243-256

Akuoko-Asibey, A. (1997) 'Views of selected government officials on the impact of a rural water supply and sanitation program in Ghana.' *Evaluation and Program Planning* 20:225-230

Ampofo, J. A. (1997) 'A survey of microbial pollution of rural domestic water supply in Ghana.' *International Journal of Environmental Health Research* 7:121-130

Asante, F., Engel, S., and M. Iskandarani (2002) Water Security in the Ghanaian Volta Basin. Patterns, determinants, and consequences. *Quarterly Journal of International Agriculture* 41:145-167

Bacho, F. Z. L. (2001a) *Infrastructure delivery under poverty. Potable water provision through collective action.* SPRING, Dortmund.

Bacho, F. Z. L. (2001b) *From a gift of nature to an economic good: Changing perceptions and management of drinking water.* SPRING, Dortmund

Botchway, K. (2001) 'Paradox of empowerment. Reflections on a case study from Northern Ghana.' *World Development* 29:135-153

Botchway, K. (2004) *Understanding 'development' interventions in Northern Ghana. The need to consider political and social forces necessary for transformation.* Edwin Mellen Press, Lewinston

Carbone, T. (2004) *Probleme der Trinkwasserverteilung in ländlichen Haushalten Ghanas - dargestellt am Beispiel des Volta-Beckens.* Diplom Thesis, Geographisches Institut der Rheinischen Friedrich-Wilhelm-Universität Bonn

Destombes, J. (1999) *Nutrition and economic destitution in Northern Ghana, 1930-1957. A historical perspective on nutritional economics.* Working Paper 49/99

Doe, S. R. and M. S.Khan (2004) 'The boundaries and limits of community management. Lessons from the water sector in Ghana.' *Community Development* 49:360-371

Eguavoen, I. (2007) *Now, you have a pump, you have to manage it. Household water management, water rights and institutional change in Northern Ghana.* PhD Thesis, Institut für Völkerkunde, Universität Köln

Engel, S., Iskandarani, M., and M. Del Pilar Useche, (2005) 'Improved water supply in the Ghanaian Volta Basin: Who uses it and who participates in community decision-making?' *EPT Discussion paper* 129, IFPRI, Washington DC

Engel, S., M. Iskandarani and M. Del Pilar Useche (Forthcoming) 'Household water security in the Ghanaian Volta Basin: Why do people still not use improved water sources?' *Journal of River Basin Management*

Fuest, V. (2006) 'Ethnologie in der Arena.' *Sociologus,* 56 (1):37-67

Galla, S. Z. and B. R.. Bandie (2004) 'Pump management committees and sustainable community water management in the Upper West and East Regions of Ghana.' *Ghana Journal of Development Studies* 1:72-90

GVP homepage: www.glowa-volta.de

Hunter, J. M. (1992) 'Elephantiasis: a disease of development in North East Ghana.' *Social Science and Medicine* 35:627-649

Hunter, J. M. (1997a) 'Boreholes and the vanishing of Guinea worm disease in Ghana´s Upper Region.' *Social Science and Medicine* 45: 71-89

Hunter, J. M. (1997b) 'Geographical patters of Guinea worm infestation in Ghana: an historical contribution.' *Social Science and Medicine* 44:103-122

Iskandarani, M., Berger, T., Laube, W., and Y. Osei-Asare (2002) GLOWA Volta Household Survey. Documentation of the Questionnaire. ZEF document. URL: www.glowa-volta.de

Karikari, K. (1996). 'Water supply and management in rural Ghana: overview and case studies.' In: E. Rached, E. Rathgeber, and D. B. Brooks (eds.) *Water Management in Africa and the Middle East. Challenges and Opportunities.* IDRC, Ottawa

Kendie, S. B. (1992) 'Survey of water use behaviour in rural North Ghana.' *Natural Resources Forum* May:126-131

Kendie, S. B. (1996) 'Some factors influencing effective utilization of drinking water facilities: women, income, and health in rural North Ghana.' *Environmental Management* 20:1-10

Kendie, S. B. (1999) *Water supply, sanitation and hygiene. Analysis of connecting factors in Northern Ghana.* Development and Project Planning Centre, Bradford.

Kendie, S. B. and Abane, A. M. (2001) 'User committees and sustainable development of drinking water services in Rural Northern Ghana.' In: Y. Saaka (ed.) *Regionalism and Public Policy in Northern Ghana.* Peter Lang, New York and Frankfurt, pp 177-201

Laube, W., Van de Giesen, N. (2006) 'Ghana water law and policy: Institutional issues and hydrological perspectives.' In: J.S. Wallace, P. Wouters, and S. Pazvakavambwa (eds.) *Hydrological information in water law and policy: current practice and future potential.* Water Policy Series, Kluwer

McNeill, D. (1999) On interdisciplinary research: with particular reference to the field of environment and development. *Higher Education Quarterly,* 53(4):312-329

Mensah, K. (1998) Restructuring the delivery of clean water to rural communities in Ghana: the institutional and regulatory issues. *Water Policy* 1:383-395

Mensah, K. (1999) *Water law, water rights and water supply (Africa): Ghana - study country report.* DFID Cranfield University, Silsoe.

Mollinga, P.P. (2006) *The rational organisation of dissent. Interdisciplinarity in the study of natural resources management.* Background paper for the ZEF PhD Interdisciplinary Course, Bonn

Osei-Asare, Y. (2005) *Household water security and water demand in the Volta Basin of Ghana.* Peter Lang, Frankfurt Main

Rodgers, C., Van de Giesen, N., Laube, W., Vlek, P. L. G., and E. Youkhana (2007a) 'The GLOWA Volta Project. A framework for water resources decision-making and scientific capacity building in a transnational West African basin.' *Water Resources Management* 21:295-313

Rodgers, C., Vlek, P.L.G., Eguavoen., I. and C. Arntz, (2007b) *GLOWA Volta. Phase II completion report.* ZEF, Bonn

Rosen, S. and Vincent, J.R. (1999) Household water resources and rural productivity in Sub-Sahara Africa: A review of evidence. *Development Discussion Paper* 673, Harvard Institute for International Development, Harvard

Thompson, J. et al (2001) *Drawers of water II. 30 years of change in domestic water use and environmental health in east Africa.* International Institute for Environment and Development, London

Webb P. and M. Iskandarani (1998) 'Water insecurity and the poor: Issues and research needs.' *ZEF – Discussion Papers On Development Policy* 2, Bonn

ZEF/ GVP (1999) *Sustainable water se under changing land use, rainfall reliability and water demands in the Volta Basin.* Project proposal, Bonn

ZEF/ GVP (2002). *GLOWA Volta phase II. From concepts to application.* Project proposal, Bonn

ZEF/GVP (2005a) *Endbericht Glowa Volta Phase I.* Project report, Bonn

ZEF/ GVP (2005b) *GLOWA Volta phase III. Synthesis and transfer.* Project proposal, Bonn

# 7

# Working in Fields as Fieldwork

## *Khashar*, participant observation and the *Tamorka* as ways to access local knowledge in rural Uzbekistan

### Caleb Wall

## 1. The challenges of fieldwork in Khorezm

Rural Uzbekistan is a difficult place to conduct field research. Practical difficulties are made worse by a government that seeks to restrict the activities of foreign researchers and which frightens local respondents into 'politically correct' answers, in line with state ideology. In 2005 these problems multiplied following a reported state sponsored massacre in Andijan. These challenges are exacerbated when the topic of research touches on agriculture, which remains a highly sensitive and contested issue due to the primacy that the Uzbek state places on cotton & wheat production as a mechanism of 'controlling the countryside'. For my research on local knowledge in Uzbekistan I spent a year living in a rural village (*kishlak*) in the Khorezm region, attempting to understand the local agricultural system from the perspective of the 'insider' (see Wall, 2006a & 2006b). This I achieved with a variety of methods, yet I found participatory methods particularly useful, including having my own small plot (*tamorka*[1]).

Accessing local knowledge was methodologically challenging for several reasons. First, because of the political influence over agriculture, especially cotton and wheat cultivation, farmers often presented the official method rather than the reality. Thus discussing 'politically correct' knowledge rather than 'actual' knowledge. In a country where there is a deliberate political climate of fear, respondents were cautious in how they answered questions – and an element of distrust permeated all my social relations (although this reduced over time). Second, for 'simple' forms of knowledge such as seed selection and sharing, the answers seemed so obvious to participants that interviews often failed and I was forced to adopt different approaches which were more observational in nature. As so much local knowledge is tacit, un-spoken and unrecognised, it was often difficult to know what knowledge existed or how to discuss it, as most respondents are unaware that they pos-sessed 'local knowledge' in a way that an outsider would define it. I placed particular emphasis on participatory methods, especially in establishing my own household plot (*tamorka*) and playing an active role in community work events (*khashar*)[2]. On reflection I find that how one situates oneself as a re-searcher in rural Khorezm has a considerable influence on the outcomes of the research. Given that I was trying to study how agricultural knowledge was 'managed' by its users, by the state and by a project of which I was part, the understanding I gained of local knowledge was of course situational. By posi-tioning myself at a low, local village level I was not seen as a useful 'resource' for elites, in a way that other researchers have discussed (Trevisani, 2008). This made accessing this group more difficult, yet yielded benefits in my re-search on local knowledge. Yet there is no way to escape entirely from the limitations of being a young, male, western researcher in Uzbekistan, espe-cially in researching gender issues but also in accessing some data, given the respect accorded to age and experience. What was possible was to use par-ticipatory methods as a way of breaking down some of the barriers that ex-isted.

## 2. The approach and subjectivity

The fundamental approach of my research was to use participatory methods, in order to see agricultural knowledge in Khorezm from the perspective of the 'insider'. By adopting the role of a participating observer the aim was to examine local knowledge systems in Khorezm, Uzbekistan[3]. In this paper I report on the methods used to access the 'local' knowledge system in Khorezm, distinct from the 'knowledge governors' and the 'ZEF/UNESCO' project in which I also worked[4]. This was achieved using a wide range of mainly qualitative methods, verified using some quantitative tools. Overall, the approach taken can be roughly described as the 'extended case study method', an approach "which deploys participant observation to locate eve-ryday life in its extra-local and historical context ... a reflexive model of sci-ence that takes as its premise the inter-subjectivity of scientist and subject of study" (Burawoy, 1998: 4). With none of the subject groups was I ever an objective 'fly on the wall' (Bernard, 1994: 139), observing actions in an en-tirely uninvolved manner, such an approach is simply not feasible for as con-spicuous a person as a Western researcher in Khorezm, Uzbekistan.

By choosing to live in a rural community some distance was gained from the ZEF project in which I worked, whilst concurrently winning increased levels of empathy (or at least curious bemusement) from the rural farming group. I would not seek to claim that I "went native" in the manner proposed by Kuhn, when: "one must go native, discover that one is thinking and working in, not simply translating out of, a language that was previously foreign" (Kuhn, 1996: 204). Indeed, 'going native' in the classical sense of anthropology would have been infeasible given that three distinct informant groups were studied, nor is this any longer the universally accepted aim of anthropology. Potentially, it would have been possible for the local knowledge system, yet I was reluctant to study only local knowledge in Khorezm given the interlinkages with the state plan and state order system. Rather I focused on several groups and attempted to collate data from various sources, in an attempt to understand how local knowledge was created, shared, stored and used. Certainly in Uzbekistan there were very real problems in accessing reliable data. I am certain that informants lied to me in some circumstances, many interviewees certainly obfuscated their answers and most informants were, to put it civilly, frugal with the truth.

Much of this subjectivity is driven by the particular difficulties of working in rural Uzbekistan. The nature of the state is one of political repression[5], which is exercised in a capillary manner in rural Khorezm. At the centre, in Tashkent, the state operates by governing almost every arena of public, private and economic life. The primacy of the state over personal choices (e.g. the requirement for internal travel permission), political choices[6] and economic activity leaves few opportunities for the development of a civil society. A large police and military force acts as a guarantor of the state and the tactics of these security forces regularly include intimidation, torture, sexual abuse and allegations have been made of extra-judicial killings[7]. At a local level, people are not necessarily aware of the extent of alleged state brutality yet they are certainly conscious of the risks associated with dissent. For example, after the reported massacre of protestors in Andijan many in my village were aware of a disturbance, yet ignorant of the details, but this still led to some of my contacts becoming more cautious in dealing with me. Often this took the shape of interviewees providing 'politically correct' answers, rather than discussing the reality, which is an understandable self protection strategy. What the Uzbek political situation also seemed to do is lead to the reproduction of authoritarian modes of control, at almost every level of local society. So local authorities tend to be unaccountable and hold a specific type of rational/bureaucratic power as a result of their control over agricultural knowledge (and other forms, outside of my research). Thus, these authorities prevent local experimentation or innovation, because it threatens their power position. From a research perspective, many respondents are therefore cautious about discussing their own experimentation or innovation, a primary objective of my research.

This left me in the situation whereby I had to make judgements on the basis of the validity or truthfulness of certain responses. These judgements are made by every researcher in every situation, yet the extremity of state control and induced political fear in Uzbekistan made this concern more acute in my research. These decisions were based, as best as possible, upon triangulation and cross checking. Nevertheless, I made judgements, as a researcher that no doubt had a bearing on the outcomes of this research. For instance I placed less emphasis on cotton production, which, despite its primacy for the state – was a less 'rich' source of evidence and research data. Moreover, it is very difficult for the reader of my research to be certain that these judgements and the conclusions I draw, are based upon 'hard' evidence. "Because it is difficult to know whether ethnographic statements are based on anything more than personal impressions, many ethnographies are convincing only to the degree that the ethnographer has mastered rhetoric" (Aunger, 1995: 97). Similar questions can justifiably be raised relating to the reliability of informant accounts. In post-Communist countries such as Uzbekistan, many topics of discussion may be answered in the 'politically correct' manner, which may bear only a tenuous relationship to the 'truth'. For instance, the inter-row cropping of vegetables amongst cotton plants is illegal under state norms and interviews on this subject always led to people denying the practice, i.e. providing a *politically* correct answer. Yet the reality (as observed as a participant in the planting of these vegetables) was that the practice was widespread and, to an extent, officially tolerated, closer to a *factually* correct answer. The levels of official tolerance were often in doubt so interviewees would not explicitly admit to the practice, necessitating an observation *in flagrante delicto*. In a country as poorly governed at Uzbekistan, disinformation is present at all levels in society and it is easy for researchers to accept a convenient fiction and assemble evidence to suit this, especially if the research findings are in line with state promulgated 'truths'.

In attempting to build a perspective of local knowledge, conscious of the subjectivity that I bought to the situation, I distinguished three types of subjectivity, reasons why respondents may have modified their responses. These I labelled 'situational', 'protectionist' and 'reactive' forms of subjectivity. It is necessary to understand these responses by informants in order to explain why the participatory approach was adopted.


## *Situational*

The first form of subjectivity is the situational subjectivity of the respondent. When interviewed, observed or otherwise studied, any informant is representing themselves and their situation; they are not representing the entire community or respondent group. The economic, social, political and familial status of the individual will each influence their world view, which will in turn inform their "speech, their representations, the underlying codes of their discourse and behaviour, and cognitive structures or principles of action and thought" (Galibert, 2004: 458). In short their 'situation' in life will inform their response. There is of course nothing wrong with such subjectivity, it is entirely natural (to the extent that any social process is 'natural' or 'normal') and indeed can serve to elucidate issues from the various perspectives of different actors in a community. Feminist deconstructivists such as Donna Haraway (1991, chapter 9) posit that sociologists must assemble networks of "situated knowledges", which collectively inform the greater ethnology, a concept which I adapted in my work to help discuss the 'cultural context' of knowledge. So long as the researcher is aware of the situational subjectivity of each respondent, then their responses can be seen through the prism of their "lived reality" (cf. Hooks, 1989). It is not necessary for the researcher to deconstruct these lived realities, merely they must situate these realities within the society and culture which they wish to study, an expansion of the concept of *verstehen* in European sociology (Emerson, 1981: 354) which is an observational approach, situated in local reality. Reversing this concept – I was able to situate myself (and the knowledge I gleaned from the research) more from a position of a *tamorka* holder than from an external 'expert'.

Cumulatively, this 'network' of situated responses constitutes the greater society that the ethnographer seeks to study. In my work the biggest differences in situated knowledges was between those who could be roughly grouped as 'governors' and the governed. Whilst not downplaying the significant differences, the rivalries and patron/client networks within either group, those who governed and those who were governed exhibited significantly different world views. The ways in which they dealt with me as an external researcher were different. Many of the governors saw me as a potential resource, as someone who could be used to access greater wealth or power or prestige, within their existing office[8]. Thus they had a vested interest in exhibiting a certain *persona* of themselves, one which was all knowing and in possession of 'knowledge'. In one instance, when I explained that I wished to find out about farming in Khorezm for my PhD, the agronomist concerned simply said that he knew all there was to know, so I should just interview him (Field notes, 12 May 2005). Whilst partially joking, he was throughout our relationship seeking to portray himself as omniscient. This was different from the 'governed', who would also at times see me as a resource – to build their prestige and add legitimacy to their activities. Most frustratingly during the 'marriage season' of August when I was expected to appear at every wedding as a sign of their familial status, and my position was like that of a corpse at a funeral, essential for the conduct of the ceremony yet whose concerns and cares were irrelevant. This relates to a wider issue of the 'guest' in rural Uzbekistan, and the different power dynamics that this confers on the host and the guest – who is simultaneously very important yet almost entirely lacking in agency (cf. Adams, 1999). When situating the knowledge of the local community, and how their situation informs respondent accounts, there was a tendency for the rural poor to underplay their knowledge in deference to an idea of 'superior' outside knowledge and an undervaluing of their own knowledge. This led to respondents seeking to present their knowledge as unimportant or self-apparent, not requiring explanation because of its simplicity. This reflects a tendency for local knowledge to be tacit, whilst the 'superior' knowledge of the governors tended to be explicit. These two very different situational responses to interviews played a large role in informing my conception of how informal knowledge is under-valued within Khorezm, and thus why a participatory approach to accessing it was important.


### Protectionist

Respondents may also refuse to co-operate, obfuscate their answers, change the topic or simply invent stories in an attempt to protect themselves or their kin from risk. This form of subjectivity is labelled here as 'protectionist' subjectivity, where informants adopt risk management strategies in an attempt to protect themselves from harm, perceived harm or a 'loss of face'. There is a lack of literature on the refusal of informants to co-operate fully in the ethnographical enterprise, many authors focus on the responses they did receive – not on the refusals they endured. The paucity of literature probably belies the very real practical difficulties faced by ethnographers in the field. What literature does exist deals primarily with the issue of taboo – of issues that are not culturally allowed to be discussed, especially with 'outsiders'. For instance child sex abuse and incest, two forms of deviant social behaviour that inflict considerable harm on the individuals involved, yet which are poorly discussed and analysed because of the cultural 'taboo' associated with them (Durham, 1990: 187). Another example is that of witchcraft, which is often cited as a complex and secret topic, only accessed by a researcher who has achieved adequate empathy and trust with the informant community (Bernard, 1994, chapter 7). Yet in my research, and I suspect also in my colleague's work, non participation was a real problem.

In the case of Khorezm, a taboo exists on questioning or challenging the president – both because of the fear of retribution (which is strong) and also from a real level of respect for him[9]. Thus I avoided direct discussion of the president, but in discussing agriculture one is confronted with the problem that presidential politics is imbued in rural life. For example the post-1991 expansion of vegetable plots were granted by presidential decree and labelled 'presidential lands'. Equally, many of the land reform laws have been issued as presidential decrees, and in these circumstances it is difficult to delimit discussion of the president from grounded discussion of agriculture. This led to protectionist behaviour on the part of some of my informants. Interviews on cotton would often morph into recounting stories about holidays or military service in the Soviet period. Similarly, for reasons of protectionism or simple modesty, many informants did not answer certain questions, usually changing the subject or more often providing the 'official story' or 'party line' that was guaranteed to keep them out of trouble (i.e. 'life is much better after Independence', which is certainly a debatable proposition). In other cases respondents obfuscated their answers by changing the topic.

Uzbekistan is not an open society and this self-protectionist behaviour was prevalent in my research. In the field setting of Khorezm I would argue that there is a very real issue of protectionist subjectivity. The current situation[10] reflects the unfortunate history of Soviet authoritarianism, with the associated restrictions on freedom of movement, speech and education. Moreover, because my research focused on agriculture my research was inherently political. This is because of the centrality of cotton (and agriculture in general) to the exchequer, as well as the importance of improving agricultural production as a proving ground for political advancement, in the form of regional *hokims* being responsible for constant increases in cotton production. Control over the knowledge associated with cotton production is one of the key legitimating forces for the states rational control over the economy.

At the local level this means that state 'norms' (centrally determined agronomic methods) are implemented locally using threats of land loss and legal sanction. These factors all converged to make agriculture a politically sensitive topic. There was a real need for discretion by the informant community, as a mechanism of self protectionism as well as one that I was constantly had to confront in the field. I recognise now that informant interviews conducted soon after my entry into the field were conducted before a high degree of trust existed. These delivered very different results from those after trust was established. I would not claim to have fully surmounted this protective tendency, even with my very closest informants. In every interview and in every social interaction, there always remained a level of mistrust and self-protection, one which I believe exists not only for foreign researchers but even with social interactions within Uzbek and Khorezmi culture. This is part of the reason why I favour participatory observation, as it is grounded in a certain 'reality' and can less easily be subject to politically correct behaviour – although this sort of 'reactive' behaviour still exists.

### Reactive

Perhaps the most written about form of informant subjectivity is the tendency for reactivity. This is where people change their behaviour once they know they are being studied (Bernard, 1994: 141). The basic assumption in ethnography is that reactivity always occurs at some level and to some degree, however that the more time that is spent in the field site, then the lower the level of reactivity, and, "lower reactivity means higher validity of data" (Bernard, 1994: 141). Informants adopt reactive behaviour for several different reasons. For instance Le Compte attempted to study school children's' behaviour, and informed the children that she intended to write a book about them. They reacted by acting out in the style of characters on popular TV programmes, in an attempt to "make good copy" (Le Compte et al., 1993). In situations such as Uzbekistan, where local culture demands that guests be provided with everything that they request or that the host believes the guest wants, then there is a propensity for respondents to provide the answers that they think the ethnographer wants (Adams, 1999). This again can lead to researchers being presented with a convenient fiction, for which evidence is abundant, yet which is untrue. In my research this took the form of exaggerating (or simply falsifying) stories in an attempt to provide me 'good research'. Whilst this was within the Uzbek tradition of providing 'hospitality' it also often served as a cover for topics that people did not want to discuss.

It is a difficult if not impossible task for the research to 'decipher' and then 'reconstruct' the informants' accounts, while still retaining the 'actor's perspective' at the core of the research (Emerson, 1981: 355) and doing so is fraught with risks of missing or misinterpreting an important issue, a danger in all forms of research (which are all necessarily partial) yet one more often levelled against qualitative than quantitative data. Thus I focused much more on minimising the reactivity shown by informants and much less on deconstructing people's responses. The first way I achieved this is by spending adequate time in the field to ensure that I became as much a part of normal life as possible. I did this in, the perhaps naïve opinion, that informants will seldom 'act' for the researcher indefinitely. Secondly, interviews and other forms of 'prompted' data were verified by examining 'unprompted' data such as observation of human activities and actions (cf. Galibert, 2004: 461). In this way I recognised that it was impossible to prevent reactivity, however I progressed on the assumption that it is reasonable for the researcher to lessen the impact through spending more time in the field and through a proper cross checking of data. This is where actual participation in the local knowledge system became essential. By being a part of everyday agricultural activity, it was harder for informants to mislead or misinform me. I explain in the next two sections how my field work tried to manage the risks of subjectivity.

## 3. Participatory 'field' work – The *tamorka*

In order to understand the local knowledge system, I first set out to participate in it, especially at the field level. In a sense much of the early fieldwork I undertook was quite literally that – working in agricultural fields. This included establishing a *tamorka*, a household vegetable plot to supply myself with food, but more importantly to be able to seek advice and knowledge on how to plant it. This feigned ignorance[11] served as a very useful entry into the field and did much to assuage political concerns about my presence in a village. I also found it a useful way through which I could conduct and enrich interviews, contributing much to the outcome (and enjoyment) of my field research. Because I was studying local agricultural knowledge, my own knowledge and experience was not an asset. On the contrary it was best to assume ignorance on my part and to be involved in the local knowledge system as someone who was there to learn.

## The *argorod* as an introduction

Upon entering the field, I made use of my '*tamorka*' plot of 0._2 ha attached to my house. This attempt to understand agricultural knowledge at the most immediate and household level turned out to be incredibly rewarding, both professionally and personally[12]. From a professional research perspective it served as perhaps the best way of introducing my motivations to the community. Rather than entering the field with an agenda for what I wanted to teach or provide, instead I was deliberately making myself reliant upon the help and advice of the local community. This very quickly broke down barriers between those who had been suspicious of me and my work; it also reduced any concept that I was a 'westerner' with superior knowledge. On the contrary, I was reduced to asking the simplest questions. At times this deliberate (occasionally feigned) ignorance was met with disbelief and good humour. My not knowing how wide to make the seed beds for watermelons was almost a community joke. Interestingly, a newspaper report was written about me in my first month in the community. One of the quotes from the paper was from a neighbour of mine, who said "we do not know why he has come here – he is young and has prospects, he doesn't have to live in the village. It is strange that he has chosen to live here" this probably reflects some of the confusion as to what I was doing in the village, in this regard having the *tamorka* positioned my entry as one of learning.

The *tamorka* also aided a great deal in the early stages of building personal relationships with Bemat, my key informant and local supervisor, as well as a range of other individuals who came to roffer advice, knowing it was welcome (Interview, April 7, 2005). The usefulness of the approach was reinforced on one occasion when the police visited, they asked us what we were doing and Bemat was able to answer "they grow potatoes, and tomatoes, some carrots … oh, and two sheep and some chickens", diffusing the situation with humour. In retrospect, having the *tamorka* also equipped me better for conducting research as I went into more formal interviews with knowledge governors and local farmers, armed with an awareness of what was actually occurring and was thus less liable to be fooled by convenient myths or the 'politically correct' answer because the combination of observational and interview approaches allowed for the cross-checking of data. I was able to relate my own difficulties in interviews, which built empathy with respondents. Subsequent to my research, I realised that this should not be surprising. For instance Emerson (1981) argues that active participation by the ethnographer is the key means of integration into the community, generating a richness of observational data and insight (Emerson, 1981: 351). Yet the benefits of participation are often lacking in the literature.

Participating in the local knowledge system by having my own *tamorka* also provided me with research topics that I might otherwise have missed, such as the risks associated with animal health. A topic I became aware of when six of my chickens died during my first month in the village in which I worked. The fact that my neighbours lost all their chickens to disease might well have passed unnoticed had it not been for my practical integration into this aspect of rural life. Yet it was not only a way of opening avenues for research, having a *tamorka* was in fact a methodology in of itself. The real benefit however is in reversing the normal power balance, with outsiders as richer and possessing 'superior' knowledge – with me this was clearly not the case and this helped, though did not completely achieve, a balancing of power between the researcher and respondents. Such participation also justi-fies to an extent the researcher's requests for voluntary assistance in conduct-ing interviews. Furthermore, field work creates a greater level of understand-ing by the researcher of the hardships and challenges faced in everyday life. In rural Uzbekistan these hardships are considerable and empathy is best built by direct experience. This is why I argue that 'field work' is a task that should be engaged in by all rural researchers, and has the potential to be more effec-tive in eliciting responses than traditional methods.

### Seeds – a successful semi-structured interview

In attempting to glean useful anthropological data from my *tamorka* experi-ence, I made use of semi-structured interviews. Semi-structured interviews were the principal method of data collection in my research on local knowl-edge, a common situation for the ethnographic method (Bernard et al., 1986: 383). In the extended case study of seeds, unstructured interviews, in all their different guises, played a primary role in gathering data. In essence an un-structured interview is a very informal method of research, where I as the interviewer would suggest an opening topic, then allow the respondent to answer the question in the way they wish to (cf. Rubin and Rubin, 1995). This allowed the respondent to speak about topics of interest to them, rather than answering questions on topics that are of specific interest to me as an inter-viewer. The big benefit of this is that it removes a degree of interviewer bias, in terms of which questions are asked and how they are asked. Perhaps most importantly it leaves open avenues of enquiry that were previously discounted by, or simply unknown to me as the researcher. Given that these interviews were often occurring in the context of physical work, I was often in the situation of being 'taught' how to perform a particular task, thus also gaining insight into the knowledge sharing (teaching) aspects of the local knowledge system.

One good example of how this approach worked (and where interviews did not) was in comparing my experiences of new potato varieties, introduced by a foreign NGO working in the Khorezm region. In my research I planted the improved seed potatoes in collaboration with three 'key informants' (in reality local contacts) – whereas the NGO in question conducted interviews, conducted training and delivered the seed potatoes. In this instance the seed potatoes provided were much larger than those typically used locally, which resulted in farmers cutting them in half or quarters, drying them for a day and then planting, which drastically reduced yields, yet was the local view of how best to plant the large seed potatoes. There was here an intersection of two knowledge systems; one which selects seed potatoes from the smallest (inedible) heritage seed, whilst the other is accustomed to mechanised production and using dedicated and specifically bred seed. In this way the external knowledge of the NGO is disconnected from local knowledge. The methods by which this knowledge is localised is by cutting the seed potatoes in half, a less than useful solution. Yet the NGO was unaware of this particular practice, as it is exactly the sort of thing that would not come up in an interview. The farmer would consider it too much like common sense to mention it – and the foreign NGO thought it too strange to even consider cutting seed potatoes in half. It was only through a participatory approach that this issue even arose – allowing local knowledge to be introduced into the research in a bottom-up manner.

Thus the informant speaks with their own voice, and less through the lens of the interviewer's desired information. "The strength of unstructured interviewing is that informants have great freedom to express themselves using their own cultural constructs independently of the presuppositions of the ethnographer" (Bernard et al., 1986: 384). I found that for this freedom of voice to take shape however, the interviewer must also be willing to share their own experiences and talk 'openly' and 'truthfully'. This rapport building is essential to the unstructured interview and the *tamorka* helped immensely in this regard. If respondents did not feel confident to speak, then they will not respond positively to an unstructured interview. Thus I would typically premise interviews with people I did not know, in terms of explaining why I was conducting my research and what exactly I was hoping to find out. It was here that the *tamorka* became a vast asset. An example of a particularly useful interview is when I approached a key informant and simply asked her to explain everything that she knew about collecting seeds, as *I myself needed to collect seeds*. I found this interview eminently more useful than other, abstract, interviews on the same topic. Precisely because I was setting myself up as a figure with less knowledge (and reversal of normal gender and social relations in this case) I was able to access rich ethnographic data, precisely because of my participation with the *tamorka*. This included both interviews at others' fields and *tamorka*, as well as inviting key informants to advise me on my own *tamorka*. Thus I was able to cross check responses and search for different knowledge cases from within the community.

## 4. *Khashar* and community participation

I was also an active participant in *khashar* (voluntary community activities), contributing my time and labour to community projects such as building a new cemetery wall and repairing a community building. This enabled me to observe, as a participant, how local 'masters' exercised their expert knowledge within the community and to understand how this 'mastership' was defined by the cultural context in which they operated. Continuing this in various household *khashar*, I was then able to better observe family labour dynamics as well as contribute something of value to those households who I became close to in the fieldwork period. This literal participation in the agricultural community is a rather less obtrusive manner of conducting field research. In the literature of direct observation the ideal situation is of an omnipresent 'fly on the wall' who "describes without omission or distortion all the environmental conditions of a particular field site, all the behaviour of the people there, and all their utterances" (Bernard et al., 1986: 388). This is unrealistic, not least because of the impact that a strange looking foreigner would have on the people concerned. Not to mention some serious ethical concerns. Moreover, non-participation is more likely to be 'disruptive' than participation – as it creates an abnormal situation, whereas a research participating in an event is more normal – when everyone else is participating, it is indeed strange to not participate.

In conducting *khashar* it was possible for me as a researcher to observe what occurred around me, including the rich diversity of social interactions and forms of cultural transmission that occurred, as unspoken as these are in all societies. In the instances where I used direct observation, such as with participating in building new houses, I was joining a group of men who I already knew well and related to, if not as equals, but in an equitable fashion. However, I would not overestimate the level of connection that I had to the lives of the rural poor.

> "But in spite of the cordiality and familiarity that goes hand in hand with this, no researcher is so naïve as to think that proximity leads to unconditional acceptance. Nor would this be a desirable objective." (Brennan, 1985: 8)

Regardless of the personal closeness of the observed group, direct observation necessitates the taking of precise notes. Ideally these notes should be made either during or immediately after the observation session. In my case it was almost always the latter. There are also other considerations to be taken into account when conducting a direct observation, such as the subjectivity of the respondents. As mentioned earlier in this paper, individuals tend to act differently when they know they are being observed. A partial solution to this is to spend enough time in the community so that one's presence is as least obtrusive as possible, a strategy I employed by living in the local community and only observing those individuals whom I already had relationships with. However, any ethnographer must always remember that their presence has an impact. This includes considerations of power structures at work, as well as the impact on social structures that a foreign individual brings to any group (Manias and Street, 2001: 236). In my experience this impact gradually reduced with more time spent in the field developing relationships and trust. So in the first three months in the *kishlak* I spent an average of four hours per day, five days per week conducting active observation (with a lot more passive observation and simply 'living'), which worked adequately.

Whilst behaviour was always influenced by the presence of me as an outsider, a superficial façade or act was seldom maintained in the long run. This also entailed me accepting certain limitations on what I could and could not observe a strategy of observation determined by the local culture, the subject matter and the particular attributes of the individual researcher (Clancey, 2001). This was of course always imperfect, my lack of Uzbek language and obvious strangeness of appearance[13] militated against full assimilation. Yet I still found observation a vastly rewarding source of data, especially for understanding the cultural embeddedness of knowledge in the local system. One of the better examples was being my participation in the *khashar* to build a wall for the new cemetery in my village, as well as assisting in building a mud house for the son of a key informant. This provided me with a great deal of detail in how 'masters' reproduce their knowledge within familial lines, whilst also illustrating the cultural context in which these 'masters' operated. In this example, the building of a wall for the new cemetery that was built in the Spring and Summer in my village, I joined in for several days of the '*khashar*' of men from the village, and wrote in my field notes:

> "There are effectively two work teams for the pouring of a concrete foundation for a wall. One is made up of older men and they plan the work, decide upon the boxing and the placement of the wall. The younger men all work together to make the concrete and pour it in. There is a degree of interaction down - that is that the older men help the younger and show/tell them what to do ... I am always reminded of an apprentice style of KM here in the village. Everyone knows a basic amount of 'labouring' work which can be applied in all different manners. There are also various 'experts' in the form of the master ... Collectively the group is able to get all sorts of things done, yet individually people would probably lack the range of knowledge required." (Field notes, 14 April, 2005).

I think that this example also demonstrates the cultural manner in which age and experience are respected and the notion that mastership can only be attained by experience and age, although there are instances where younger people can prove their knowledge is superior to received wisdom and thus establish their own very specialised mastership. These factors were reinforced for me, when participating in a different *khashar*, building a wall with one of my key informants. Here three generations of masters were present, along with others, and the intersection of age and mastership was reinforced (Field notes, October 2, 2005). The younger members of the *khashar* were learning a set of practical skills in a manner reminiscent of an apprenticeship. So there was a form of knowledge transfer or sharing occurring here, with the mastership being reproduced along familial lines.

But this knowledge reproduction was from the top down, with authority (and age) determining who was teacher and who was the student. It is exactly these cultural specificities that make the master a unique cultural construct within Khorezm. Whilst specialists occur in every 'knowledge society' the cultural aspect of 'authority' embeds the master into a certain power structure which exhibits certain specificities of the Khorezm region. Yet this detail of knowledge reproduction and the power relations of knowledge are exactly the sort of issue which respondents are not conscious of – and are thus unlikely to discuss explicitly in interviews. Rather this knowledge, and how it is used, is tacit – and as unspoken knowledge it can only be accessed in its use and application. Thus careful observation, as a participant, is a crucial method for accessing this form of, tacit, local knowledge. In participating in these events,

I made a deliberate decision not to 'spy' and avoided noting private or personal conversations, but rather took an active role in the *khashar* and made a point of writing detailed field notes shortly after the event. Looking back, these notes form my richest field data.

### The un-observable and un-gendered research

Yet I was not able to observe everything that occurred in my *kishlak*. Time constraints, practical difficulties and nervousness on the part of informants prevented a comprehensive picture being developed. One area, in which I was restricted from observing, and certainly from participating, was in the female, gendered, aspects of silk worm production. Silk worm production in rural Khorezm dates back to the Soviet period and is predominantly a household activity – moreover it is an agricultural activity which is rich in local knowledge and thus important for my research. Whereas the processing of the finished silk cocoons is a centralised activity, with these same central processing factories also providing 'seeds' or silk worm larvae to participating households, the rearing of worms is conducted within rural family units. Household level production entails a number of distinct tasks, which illustrate how there is a gendered distribution of certain knowledge related activities. Set out in the table below is a rough description of the processes involved in sericulture and the gender of the persons normally associated with that activity. I also rate the knowledge aspect involved, drawing on my own observations and interview data. It is important to note that my interview data and observations for this case study derive mainly from an in-depth case study of one particular household. Whilst I conducted cross-checking activities and triangulated my findings, it may be mistaken to extrapolate these results as representative for Uzbekistan.

## Table 7.1: Gendered specialisation in household silk worm production

| Task | Gender of responsible person | Level / Type of knowledge required |
|---|---|---|
| Travel to factory and purchase of larvae | Male (head of household) | Negotiating / bureaucratic ability |
| Construction of 'beds' for silk worms | Male | Basic construction |
| Laying out of paper and larvae to begin raising of worms | Female (wife of head of household) | High degree of experience |
| Cutting mulberry trees and stripping leaves for feeding to worms | Mixed (entire family) | Low skill labour |
| Spreading out of worms as they develop | Female (adult women) | Medium skill labour |
| Managing the timing of feeding and spreading of worms | Female (wife of head of household) | High degree of experience |
| Feeding of silk worms 3 - 4 times daily | Female (adult women) | Medium skill labour |
| Preparation of dry branches for silk worms to cocoon onto | Female (adult women) | Medium skill labour |
| Decision on when to harvest cocoons | Female (wife of head of household) | High degree of experience |
| Separation of cocoons from wood and cleaning of cocoons for sale | Female (large number from *kishlak*) with some men from the family | Medium skill labour |
| Sale of cocoons back to factory | Male (head of household) | Negotiating / bureaucratic ability |

The former is unremarkable in a conservative rural situation and the latter reflects a range of gendered roles related to business and financial transactions that are dominant in rural Uzbekistan. Yet what it meant for me as a male researcher was that the most interesting areas of knowledge were ones in which I could not participate. Whilst I perhaps could have made a point of insisting on participating, this would have possibly harmed my relationships with the male head of household. Moreover, it would have meant that I was having a, unjustifiable, impact on changing the events that I sought to observe. In many ways this was tempting, especially given my background in feminist and gender studies, yet I made the judgement not to insist on any disruptive participation – preferring instead participation which was understandable and acceptable to the local community.

## 5. Lessons and reflections

What I have attempted to set out in this paper is an account of what I did in Khorezm, how and why. In a sense this is how I perceive methodology, i.e. as a suite of tools that are developed and re-designed to suit the needs of the researcher in the field. Yet I would be wrong to assume that I was 'part' of the community. I was not, nor ever could be, yet I did have friends there and learnt a great deal. In explaining this, I am constantly impressed with the honesty of Sir Wilfred Thesiger:

> "I was happy in the company of these men who had chosen to <spend time> with me. I felt affection for them personally, and sympathy with their way of life. But though the easy quality of our relationship satisfied me, I did not delude myself that I could be one of them. They were Bedu and I was not; they were Muslims and I was a Christian. Nevertheless, I was their companion … a bond between host and guest" (Thesiger, 2003: 119).

This concept of host and guest is an important one in rural Uzbekistan. As a guest it is possible, and important, to participate in rural and family life. Yet as a guest this level of participation is ultimately determined by the host, who has both considerable obligations to – and control over – the guest (Adams, 1999). Thus my host was the male head of household and it would have been impolite and perhaps counterproductive, to insist on involvement in what were gendered as 'female' activities. Thus certain parts of my research on local knowledge are missing, because of the gender 'gap' in my research. Whereas the opportunities to be involved in *khashar* provided rich ethnographic data and these form much of the evidence I present in my work on local knowledge. Moreover it meant that I was able to make a, small, contribution to my host. When I participated in *khashar* it was as part of the contribution of my *joshuli*, Bemat. This elevated his social prestige (who else could bring a foreigner to a *khashar*), provided no small amount of amusement (usually related to my ignorance) and at least demonstrated a willingness (if not necessarily the ability) to contribute to the community. In the same fashion having a *tamorka* was an incredibly useful introduction to the rural community, situating me as 'ignorant' and thus rebalancing the power structure in the interview process. It also served to enrich my field research experience and opened up new avenues of enquiry to which I might otherwise have remained ignorant. It was also personally fulfilling and fun. The examples of the *tamorka*, seed interviews and various *khashar* all illustrate the benefits of a participatory approach to field research. It is not possible to act as an independent 'fly on the wall'; rather it is preferable to become actively involved wherever possible. There are of course areas in which participation is not possible, here other research approaches must be used, yet the participatory research approach is a useful one in rural Uzbekistan. Indeed, when a researcher has to surmount the obstacles of reflexivity and subjectivity, in a 'hostile' or difficult research environment, the participatory approach is well advised. Likewise, when researching 'invisible' topics like knowledge, which do not lend themselves well to interviews, participatory observation is a crucial method.

# Notes

[1] The *tamorka* (*mallak* in Khorezmi dialect) is a crucial aspect of rural livelihood strategies. They provide much of the household nutrition (in the form of vegetables and livestock) and are one of the few areas of agriculture which exist largely outside of state control. Allowed during the Soviet period and expanded significantly since 1991, the *tamorka/argorod* is very much the fruit and vegetable basket for the rural poor. Significantly, keeping a *tamorka* is seen as an activity for the poor – the European fad for 'allotment' gardening amongst the middle classes would be nonsensical in Khorezm. Not keeping a *tamorka* establishes a family as wealthy enough to avoid physical labour and to buy in their food requirements.

[2] Several transliteration systems persist. Alternative spellings include: *tomorqa*, in Uzbek (Cyrillic) томорқа and *hashar*, in Uzbek (Cyrillic) ҳашар.

[3] The systems approach to understanding knowledge can be defined as determining how "knowledge is created, shared, stored and used' in a specific location (Wall, 2006a)

[4] This is a large, on-going interdisciplinary research project in rural Uzbekistan, operated by my employer at the time, the Center for Development Research at Bonn University, Germany. Project website: www.khorezm.uni-bonn.de

[5] "Uzbekistan is a non-democratic regime. The country's constitution provides for a presidential system with a formal separation of powers among the executive, legislative, and judicial branches. It also sets forth guarantees of fundamental civil rights. In practice, however, the executive branch, under the leadership of President Islam Karimov, dominates all aspects of political life. It exercises extensive control over civil society, religious groups, political parties and movements. Opposition parties are systematically denied registration. Media freedom is nonexistent. The judiciary is not independent. Torture is widespread in the country's pre-trial and post-conviction facilities. The economic system has hardly been reformed since the Soviet period. It lacks any orientation to a market economy." (BTI, 2005).

[6] "Independent opposition political parties such as Erk and Birlik were unsuccessful in registering ahead of the 26 December [2005] parliamentary election." Amnesty International (web.amnesty.org/report2005/uzb-summary-eng)

[7] This approach has, however, been manifesting itself in the common and persistent use of torture as a means of obtaining confessions, using such methods as "suffocation, electric shock, rape and other sexual abuse" (State Department, 2002: 3). Indeed, it is estimated that some 7,500 intellectuals, Islamic "fundamentalists", and other individuals were incarcerated without charge during 2003. Human Rights Watch (2001) notes that "Police and local authorities also organized 'hate rallies' reminiscent of the Stalin era, in which hundreds of neighbours and officials gathered to denounce publicly relatives of pious Muslims as traitors and 'enemies of the state' and to demand a vow of contrition" (p.5). Islam Karimov, President during the Soviet period and recently confirmed for his third term, retains control of all levels of state apparatus.

[8] For instance when I attended a *pakaz* or farming demonstration organised by the deputy mayor (who arrived in an embarrassingly large Chevrolet, testament to the success of the cotton crop) my presence as a 'foreign expert'

which I certainly was not, was used to legitimate the demonstration (Wall, 2006a: 130)

[9] This view of the president as a 'good man' surrounded by incompetent and corrupt advisors, on whom the blame falls, seemed prevalent in rural Khorezm. I label it 'Long live the King, Death to his Ministers'

[10] Discussed at length in Lewis (2005), March (2003)

[11] I was not as ignorant of agriculture as I initially portrayed. Where it was useful for me to demonstrate my knowledge and usefulness, I was generally able to do so. As one colleague commented on an earlier draft "if you had been a 'tiny academic' you would not have been taken that seriously either … physical strength matters and creates respect and authority" in this regard my ability to work the land by hand and contribute to the heavier parts of *khashar*, were also important – as was a basic knowledge of agronomy.

[12] I am indebted to my colleague Gert Jan Veldwisch for his help and support during my time in the field – the tamorka was as much mine as it was his – although it was perhaps more central to my research topic. Likewise my *joshuli* in Khorezm, Bemat, made having the *tamorka* possible and I owe the success of my field research to his support.

[13] At over six feet tall with red hair – I am not the most usual sight in rural Khorezm.

# References

Adams, L. L. (1999) 'The mascot researcher: identity, power, and knowledge in fieldwork.' *Journal of Contemporary Ethnography* 28(4):331-363

Aunger, R. (1995) 'On ethnography: storytelling or science?' *Current Anthropology* 36(1):97-130

Bernard, H. R. (1994) *Research methods in anthropology: qualitative and quantitative approaches.* Sage Publications, Thousand Oaks, CA

Breman, J (1985) 'Between accumulation and immersion: The partiality of fieldwork in rural india.' *Journal of Peasant Studies* 13:5-36

BTI - *Bertelsmann Transformation Index* (2005) URL: www.bertelsmann-transformation-index.de/151.0.htm

Burawoy, M. (1998) 'The extendend case method.' *Sociological Theory,* 16(1):4-33

Clancey, W. J. (2001) 'Field science ethnography: methods for systematic observation on an arctic expedition.' *Field Methods* 12:223-243

Durham, W. H. (1990) 'Advances in evolutionary culture theory.' *Annual Review of Anthropology* 19:187-211

Emerson, R. (1981) Observational field work. *Annual Review of Sociology* 7:351-378

Galibert, C. (2004) 'Some preliminary notes on actor-observer Anthropology.' *International Social Science Journal* 56(181):455-467

Haraway, D. (1991) *Simians, cyborgs and women.* Routledge, New York

Hooks, B. (1989) *Talking back: thinking feminist, thinking black.* South End Press, Boston

Kuhn, T. (1996) *The structure of scientific revolutions.* Third edition. University of Chicago Press, Chicago

LeCompte, M. D., Preissle, J. and R. Tesch (1993) *Ethnography and qualitative design in educational research.* Second edition. Academic Press, Orlando, FL

Lewis, D. (2005) *Uzbekistan: rigged elections in a surreal land.* Transitions Online, (01/04/2005)

Manias, E. and Street, A. (2001) 'Rethinking ethnography: reconstructing nursing relationships.' *Journal of Advanced Nursing* 33(2):234-242

March, A. (2003) 'State ideology and the legitimation of authoritarianism: the case of post-Soviet Uzbekistan.' *Journal of Political Ideologies* 8(2):209-232

Rubin, H. J. and I. S. Rubin (1995) *Qualitative interviewing: the art of hearing data.* Sage, Newbury Park

State Department, United States Department (2002) *Uzbekistan country reports on human Rights Practices 2001.* Released by the Bureau of Democracy, Human Rights, and Labor. March 4, 2002 URL: www.state.gov/g/drl/rls/hrrpt/2001/eur/8366.htm

Thesiger, Wilfred (2003) *My life and travels.* Flamingo, London

Trevisani, T. (2008, forthcoming) *Changing patterns of land control in Uzbekistan: agricultural policies, dynamics of power and social conflict in and after the kolkhozes of Khorezm.* PhD thesis, FU Berlin, Institute for Ethnology

Wall, C. (2006a) *Knowledge Management in Rural Uzbekistan: Peasant, Project and Post-Socialist Systems of Knowledge in Khorezm.* PhD thesis in the Philosophy Faculty, Bonn University, URL: hss.ulb.uni-bonn.de/diss_online/ phil_fak/2006/wall_caleb

Wall, C. (2006b) 'Managing Local and External Knowledge in a Development Research Project in Uzbekistan.' *Knowledge Management for Development,* 2(3): 111-122 www.km4dev.org/journal/index.php/km4dj/article/ viewFile/78/197

# 8

# *Authoritarianism, Validity, and Security*
## Researching water distribution in Khorezm, Uzbekistan

### G.J.A. Veldwisch

## 1. Introduction

This chapter discusses difficulties and practicalities associated with conducting field research on a politically sensitive topic. I discuss the research methodology adopted for my doctoral research on irrigation management in the Khorezm region of Uzbekistan, but at a second level the chapter addresses the wider issues of conducting research on the organisation of agriculture and water management in rural Uzbekistan.

In Uzbekistan water is mainly used for agriculture, which is still strongly controlled by the state, especially in connection to cotton production. Water distribution is therefore highly connected to this state controlled agricultural production. For that reason the study of water distribution in Uzbekistan is in effect also the study of the political economy of agriculture in general, and that of cotton production in particular. A report by the International Crisis Group (2005) discusses the connections between the authoritarian regime and the current organisation of the cotton economy[1].

> "Millions of the rural poor work for little or no reward growing and harvesting the crop. The considerable profits go either to the state or small elites with powerful political ties. Forced and child labour and other abuses are common" (ICG, 2005: i).

Structural economic reform could undermine the lucrative business of the people in command and eventually become a threat to their political power.[2] As a result the study of water distribution and agricultural production is a sensitive affair with challenges regarding the security of participants and the validity of the results.

The basic methodological elements of my doctoral research are summarised in Table 8.1 below. Methodology can conceptually be understood as consisting of three levels; (1) the scientific model, which constitutes the epistemological and ontological foundation of the research (2) the research method or strategy, and (3) the research techniques (Burawoy 1998: 6; Alasuutari, 1995; Bryman, 2004).

**Table 8.1 – Three levels of methodology as applied in the research**

| | *Basic elements of this study* | *Difficulties encountered* | *Emphases and adaptation made in response to difficulties* |
|---|---|---|---|
| *Scientific model* | Critical realist; reflexive; making use of constructivist and Actor Network Theory concepts regarding technology | No social science history in former Soviet Union; lack of fitting theories; little contextual info; many problems in 'objectively' abstracting information | Focus on identifying mechanisms; engage rather than remain at a distance; develop theory rather than test existing; an integrated approach to the social and material dimension. |
| *Research method/strategy* | Extended case method; mix-method triangulation; technography | Issues not clear; lack of fitting theories; | Theoretical sampling; strong focus on empirical grounding; riddle solving/ defining integrated in the research process |
| *Research techniques* | (Participant) observations, household survey; non/semi-structured interviews; group interviews; field note diaries; acquisition of secondary data; | High levels of distrust, unreliable statistics, | Building rapport/ finding out slow; combine interviews with observations; acquire secondary data at field level; |
| (including strategic choices of operation) | learning Uzbek, live in a village, own transport | huge area/large distances, difficult language, no good research assistants | learn Uzbek and live in a village + project's guest house; make use of my role as outsider and irrigation engineer. |

The way each level is "filled-in" is related to choices at the other levels. There is (or should be) coherence between the scientific model, the research strategy and the research techniques, though there are no simple one-to-one relations between levels. With some adaptations and/or changed emphases, strategies and techniques of a certain scientific model can also made to fit other scientific models. In the third column of the table I have listed the main difficulties encountered in conducting the research. Also the issues at the different levels are somewhat interlinked; the post-soviet authoritarian regime resulted in the absence of a social science counterpart and a lack of relevant (applied) theories on the topic of research (first level), the absence of (empirically based) information to formulate reasonable hypotheses (second level) as well as high levels of distrust among the population and the absence of reliable secondary data (third level).

Though in the first half year of the research an approach was developed that took into account the expected challenges, in the course of the research process adaptations were made at each level in response to difficulties/situations encountered in reality. Not always were these conscious choices. There were also de facto implications of certain ways of doing that were followed for pragmatic reasons. The methodology of the PhD research is the result of three years designing and developing an appropriate methodological approach for this challenging environment and politically sensitive topic of research.

Methodology concerns the entire research process, which consists of several phases. They can for instance be described as research design, data collection, analysis, interpretation and write-up. In practice these 'phases' are not always clearly distinguishable, neither as time periods nor as activities. In this study different phases and functions were explicitly integrated. This is evident in the relation between defining the topic, formulating the research questions, production of observations, documenting of observations and processing them. All of this is an iterative, fluid process of going back and forth between theory and empirical material. The process of analysis, or unriddling, did not wait until after the fieldwork. Rather, it is an integral part of the field research process and of the preparation process (through reading existing material and formulating tentative research questions and hypotheses). Towards the end of the second year of fieldwork the main idea for the dissertation had already ripened. In my experience, the exercise of riddle solving in the first place is a creative process; unstructured writing, active brainstorming, discussing with colleagues and silent pondering all played a role in this ripening process. At the same time it required discipline in field note taking and systematic ordering of ideas that were taking shape during the fieldwork period.

The paper first discusses the three levels of methodology identified above in sections 2 to 4. All three sections address the reasons for the initially adopted methods/approaches as well as practical examples of adaptation. Section 5 methodologically evaluates the research, resulting in the formulation of some principles for an effective strategy/methodology to conduct social science research in contemporary Uzbekistan.

## 2. The scientific model

The scientific model underlying the water management research can be characterised as critical realist with an interaction process between the theoretical and the empirical that could be called 'retroductive'. It is different from both positivist and interpretative epistemologies and is neither deductive nor inductive in its organisation of theory and observations. Critical realism builds on the idea that there is a real world 'out there', but that we only know it through the constructions that people make of it. The objects of science, the things that we study (physical processes or social phenomena) form the intransitive dimension of science; the theories and discourses of science are part of its transitive dimension (Sayer, 2000:10). Critical realism distinguishes between the real, the actual and the empirical. The real refers to the structural possibilities as they exist, whereas the actual refers to the way in which things happen. Forces have different effects, that is: there is no linear relation between cause and effect. Rather the mechanisms of change need to be studied in-depth in order to understand social processes of change.

This process of analysis is like solving a riddle (Alasuutari, 1995: 6-22) i.e. fitting all the clues together in a logical way. Critical realists advocate retroduction as a logic for moving between the empirical and theory. Retroduction goes through a "mode of inference in which events [the empirical, GJAV] are explained by postulating (and identifying) mechanisms which are capable of producing them" (Sayer, 1992).

The extended case method has a similar aim; it "applies reflexive science to ethnography in order to extract the general from the unique, to move from the 'micro' to the 'macro' ..." (Burawoy, 1998: 5). Burawoy (ibid: 27) argues for a more prominent role of existing theory in the research process; "the analyst works with a prior body of theory that is continually evolving through attention to concrete cases. Theory is reconstructed." The researcher oscillates between theory and observations; theory guides the direction of fieldwork and observations redirect theory. This is different from for instance grounded theory, which ideally starts purely from observations and builds theory from systematically working with the produced empirical material. Also Alasuutari (1995) emphasizes the importance of starting with empirical observations and move towards the development of theory, rather than starting with a theory and/or hypothesis and testing or verifying it through fieldwork.

This specific vision on the fundamental relation between the empirical and theory requires research strategies that provide for the possibilities of being guided by the instances in the field or for possibilities of moving between them.

The topic of my PhD research, agrarian change and the socio-political aspects of irrigation management in post-independence Uzbekistan was part of a largely unexplored field of work. Therefore there was a greater scope for theory development than for theory testing; there are good opportunities for theory refinement and reconstruction. Also, neither during the Soviet period nor in the period after independence social sciences have been established in Uzbekistan. Almost all relevant studies conducted in the field are by foreign researchers or by Uzbeks at foreign universities. As a result a natural Uzbek counterpart institute for the social science component of the ZEF/UNESCO project was lacking.

The object of the research is an irrigation network. Elsewhere this has also been called a 'water network' (Van der Zaag et al., 2002; Bolding, 2004; Veldwisch et al., forthcoming). As in actor-network theory (ANT), the network is understood to be of heterogeneous nature, i.e. human and non-human (social and technical) elements are woven together (Callon, 1991; Latour 1991). The research builds on the notion that the social and the technical are different dimensions of the same processes.

The above has several methodological implications, which are elaborated in the following two sections.

# 3. The research approach

## *Basic elements*

The objective of the research was to contribute analytical descriptions of the processes at play in water distribution in Khorezm. The research approach that was adopted focused on identifying the mechanisms of social and political change as expressed in the management of natural and technological processes. Good analytic case studies of agrarian change processes in Central Asia are scarce, which makes it very important to first study the mechanisms of these processes before quantifying them (Kandiyoti, 1999). This is one of the important reasons for a strong focus on qualitative methods that identify such mechanisms. The absence of (applied) theories and analytic case studies also made it difficult to formulate precise research questions at the onset of the study. Based on general (not region or situation specific) theories and the (limited) available information on the research topic and research area possibly relevant issues were imagined. Working hypotheses were formulated to guide the direction of the research. During the study these hypotheses were frequently revised and renewed on basis of field observations and other data collected, and methodological choices were made on the basis of this.

In grounded theory this is referred to as theoretic sampling.

> "the process of data collecting for generating theory whereby the analyst jointly collects, codes and analyzes his data and decides what data to collect next and where to find them in order to develop his theory as it emerges" (Glaser and Strauss 1967: 45).

For example, earlier observations of and interviews with farming families and Water Users Associations (WUAs), two important units of analysis in this research (see section 5), informed the selection of subsequent cases to be studied. The theory-observation interaction also informed the choices of topics to be addressed and the choices of concrete place-time situations to be attended and observed. Selections were made to shed light on a topic or concrete situation from a different point of view, or sometimes to explore new spheres, which were touched upon in earlier fieldwork and seemed relevant for the topic under research.

Analysis was partly done by theorizing directly from observations but more commonly by interpreting encountered situations through the lenses of existing theories. An example of theorising purely from observations was the development of an understanding of the Khorezmian agrarian system to exist of three distinct forms of production with each an own specific way of securing access to irrigation water. In later stages theories were found that fitted the observations, which enriched the analysis, but the first analysis emerged purely from observations. An example where the interaction between theory and observations played an important role was the re-interpretation of how irrigation infrastructure is an expression of social relations. The specificities of (post-) Soviet collective agriculture created very different social relations around water distribution than known from literature on other parts of the world. The Soviet social relations of water distribution did not so much affect water distribution structures as signposts of struggle or material interfaces between competing farmers, a core topic in international socio-technical irrigation management research, but the relative unimportance of physical design and remodelling of infrastructure expressed the force of centralised control. The layout of the irrigation network of Khorezm and its technology can still be seen as an expression of a specific socio-political situation, an insight provided by existing theory in this field, but the concrete from of that expression could not be derived from that theory and had to be analysed anew.

### *Mixed method triangulation as a strategy*

At the start of this study the concept of triangulation was merely used as in data triangulation. That involves the cross-checking of data acquired in other situations and/or at other moments. As the checking of data often proved difficult due to reasons of sensitivity of the information, the idea of validation through triangulation was looked into in more detail. The idea of mixed method triangulation (MMT) was found to fit well to the already adopted approach. Downward and Mearman (2006) argue for mixed-method triangulation (MMT) as a prerequisite for a process of retroduction with ontological depth. They argue that combining methods that are connected to different ontological positions provides the opportunities of shifting between different interpretations of the same processes and thus generate understandings that transcend mere disciplinary perspectives. Combining of methods is a means of retroduction, which "is not so much a formalised logic of inference as a thought operation that moves between knowledge of one thing to another, for example, from empirical phenomena expressed as events to their causes" (ibid.). Therefore retroduction makes use of mechanisms and relations known from empirical study as well as theoretical relations. When in new situations aspects are recognised from earlier encountered mechanisms or relations, the similarity to earlier encountered situations or phenomena is investigated, be it through theoretical reflection or through empirical study. The explanation is suggested by "concomitance", i.e. any type of similarity or co-occurrence (Thompson, 2007). Such a relation might be a happy coincidence and therefore does not validate a conclusion in the sense that it is highly trustworthy. However, the approach makes it possible to move between different locations and informants and using the findings at one place as a hint for understanding what is happening in another situation. Practically it implied distilling working hypotheses from one specific case and testing that in other situations. As a result the processes had to be formulated more precisely and/or the situation in which the process occurred was narrowed-down. On top of that the identified processes could be further tested and quantified.

To exemplify this approach I describe one small aspect of my research and how the topic, questions, and hypotheses developed. Walking through the agricultural fields and following the canals I once came across an irrigation ditch that directly connected to a drain. A lot of water was flowing to the drain unused. In the weeks that followed I paid special attention to this phenomenon and more frequently I stopped the car at places where this might also occur, walked the extra few hundred meters to check the end of an irrigation ditch and asked various people why water was flowing to the drain unused. I came across a number of similar situations and the only reason that farmers and farm workers gave me was 'carelessness'. I hypothesised that the unused water flowing into the drains would represent a major item on the (district) water balance and that it would only be happening in case of water abundance. This led me to investigate the situation of water shortage and water abundance in more detail – the follow up I do not discuss here. Besides I started to talk about this type of water wastage to the district level water management departments and found out that this is a major point of attention for their fieldworkers, something they had not told me in earlier interviews. In about the same period I coincidentally came across a district water manager who was following a large drain to close off any unnecessary outflows of canals. I was told this was done in order to increase the efficiencies on district level to have enough water available at the tail-end of the district. This reinforced my idea that in case of water shortage this type of water wastage would not occur. Going around with a water inspector I found out that these connections were 'illegal' and that the responsible farmers were fined for this, however, not in all cases. At two places where we found water flowing to the drain further downstream it was being used again. Drains were being used as irrigation system at places that could not easily be reached by irrigation ditches. In both of these two places the water was used for paddy cultivation, which is often illegal. This could have been the reason why people were only telling me that letting water flow to the drain was due to 'carelessness'. In the subsequent weeks I systematically followed the drains that 'unnecessarily' received water from an irrigation ditch. Only in a few cases I found that the water was actually being used. In areas and periods of relative water shortage I did not find situations of this direct water loss. This was also confirmed by the words and actions of the water inspector, who only checked such connections in areas and periods of relative water abundance.

## 4. Issues regarding research methods

This section deals with a number of issues that played at the level of research techniques. It does not describe the techniques in detail, but reflects on their use.

### *Project and some strategic choices*

At the moment of starting my research (in 2004) the interdisciplinary project of which my PhD research was part was operating since about three years (since 2001). During their field work periods all researchers had been living in the project's guesthouse from where they jointly commuted to the office building at the university campus. Fieldwork was conducted in project cars, clearly marked with project logos and blue-coloured UN number plates and supplied with a driver. This mode of operation linked well to the natural science based experiments and approaches that formed the heart of the ZEF/UNESCO project during the initial years of research. It involved making long days and covering long distances with the main concern of solving practical issues. The economic research operated in similar mode, while some of social science researchers without much success struggled for a different regime.

Changing of the mode of operation for at least the social scientists gathered momentum in the period that I started the field research. Thus it was possible that, contrary to what was common, I lived in a village rather than in the project's guesthouse. During the first year of fieldwork I rented a house in a small, rural village, together with a colleague. During the second year I stayed in the same village, but then for a few nights per week in a host family. Even though most of my active fieldwork was outside the village, I frequently spent time in the village also during daytime – doing computer work at home, working in the garden or spending time relaxing with neighbours. Living in an agricultural community enabled me to observe social life and agricultural practices in a relatively unconstrained way; the longer I stayed, the less people seemed to be disturbed by my presence. Though very beneficial for my own research there was light pressure from within the project to spend more time in the office and/or the guesthouse for reasons of integration with other research team members and informal knowledge sharing.

In the first year I hired a car to go around without a driver and project car. This gave me more flexibility in deciding when and where to go. Moreover, we would only arrive with two people, instead of three, which was a bit less of an invasion. However, the travel was often long and tiresome, which after a few months made me decide to again go around with project cars and drivers.


### Entrance to the field and network building

Before I started my fieldwork various people had advised me to first get permission to do the research from the local authorities, especially from the district governor's office (*Hokimiyat*), as working without such a written permission people would not feel free to talk. Officially I did not need such permission, as our project had a 'blanket permission' to perform research on agriculture in Khorezm. Rather than working from the official offices downward, as others had done, I started with building up relations at the field level and moved my way up by getting introduction to their peers and bosses. A few people suggested to me that I should ask permission from their boss before they would talk to me, but in general it was quite possible to operate under the radar of the authorities, i.e. I was noticed, but my activities did not raise suspicion. It also helped to be explicit about where I lived and worked, mention names of people that we mutually knew and to hand over a business card that they could show in case someone would come and inquire after me.

With time the number of informants at higher positions grew, as I frequently worked in their areas of jurisdiction and with their staff. I tried to be as open as possible to these informants, in order to gain their trust. In situations where I managed to do that they instructed their staff to be co-operative as well. On the other hand I did not want to tell them explicitly with whom I had talked about what, as that could bring those people in difficulties. I was walking the narrow path of on the one hand staying both critical and making my own choices on what to do and on the other hand being open about my activities and letting me be guided by people at strategic places. I am fully aware that due to this attitude I have missed a number of interesting topics, but practically it was simply not possible to operate around these persons and yet get access to people and get reliable answers from them. In a similar way I avoided any unnecessary focus on illegal or highly sensitive issues, such as bribes. Yet, especially the paddy cultivation and the water needed for that was at the heart of my research and sometimes it was unavoidable to push a sensitive topic into the conversation.

## Distrust and participation

Is a respondent free to decide whether to participate in the research or not? In Uzbek society the guest is considered to be 'king', who can not be denied whatever is requested (Wall and Overton, 2006; Adams, 1999). When approaching people with the question whether they are willing to participate, especially as a foreigner, you are almost always instantly hosted and served the best food and drink available. It rather requires sensitivity of the guest, in this case the researcher, to assess whether the possible informant is really willing to participate. From a pragmatic point of view this also makes sense, as continuing with an informant that formally consents to participate, but in practice is not willing to talk is chasing a difficult source of information. The most important reason for not wanting to participate seemed to be fear of being negatively affected by participating. In many cases people took a protective attitude. This was one of the main difficulties encountered in conducting the research. Wall (this volume) reported similar difficulties. In interviews people often evaded questions, gave vague responses, produced plain lies or simply changed the topic. Often when people seemed to be afraid to talk it was not explicitly expressed. However, in a number of cases people hinted that the topic brought up was not appropriate to talk about, and in some cases explicitly told me so. When people did tell me about things that were obviously politically sensitive, after the interview they often asked me not to reveal the source to anyone, which made it difficult to cross-check the given account and present it as a research finding.

The decision to keep quiet about issues of dissatisfaction can be interpreted as a decision to not discredit the state and/or powerful people. This situation of extreme "loyalty" seems to be a forced one, i.e. forced by the lack of other options. Hirschman (1970) analysed three possible responses to an uncomfortable situation: exit, voice and loyalty. Most people in Uzbekistan do not have the possibility to leave their country, region or social position, nor do they have the position to voice their discontent. The only reasonable survival strategy is to accommodate, to be loyal no matter what.

During the field research I was followed and checked by people in authoritative positions (heads of state organisation, former collective farm managers, etc) or by their informants. Several people whom I interviewed mentioned that after contact with me they could be approached to ask about my research and whereabouts. In a few cases I know that this actually happened. I had the impression that people in authoritative positions would have easily been able to block the research in case they would have felt it could be a threat to their personal position or to the state. Also I was warned by two individual contacts that my work was being monitored by the secret police, though seemingly not on a very intensive basis, as my work was never openly obstructed and I could go and talk to whoever I wished.

Some topics were found to be more politically sensitive than others. Self-evidently corruption by informal payments was a sensitive topic to talk about. Some other sensitive issues were the land acquisition procedures, exact sizes and arrangements of land tenure, payment of the workers by the *fermers*, and the negotiations over crop quota. Above all, paddy cultivation is perceived as a highly sensitive issue, as it requires a lot of water, competes with cotton cultivation, is not fully legal, and provides a major source of income. When bringing up these topics a protective attitude was regularly encountered.

## Building rapport and identity

The main tactic of overcoming situations of distrust was an extra focus on the building of rapport. I tried to build up long term relations, with repeated visits in which I did not just focus on getting the data I was looking for, but also reserved plenty of time to listen and respond to the informant. The learning of the Uzbek language soon turned out a very effective tool to gain the positive attention and trust of the people. Foreigners are clearly expected to speak (or learn) Russian, not Uzbek. When I told people (in Uzbek) that I did not speak Russian, they often looked at me in disbelief. And it frequently happened that people kept speaking Russian to me even when I spoke Uzbek to them. Even though many people master basic Russian, it is perceived as the language of 'the centre'; older people, males, educated people, people from urban areas and especially if they come from Tashkent or abroad, speak Russian. Learning Uzbek helped me in shifting my bias to the people in the margin; the younger people, the women, the uneducated, and the people in the rural areas. Although I started studying the Uzbek language from the moment I arrived in the country, I never reached the level at which I could conduct interviews on my own. Therefore I permanently worked with a

translator; over the whole period I hired four different persons, who translated between English and Uzbek. In the beginning I was hardly able to have
a basic conversation, but even then it clearly helped to open up the relation.
Later my Uzbek language skills improved and sometimes I was even able to
discuss simple issues without the help of a translator. Also I was often able to
get the gist of the story even before it was translated. This helped enormously
to keep a more natural communication between me and the informants; even
when I could not speak with them directly, still it was clear that I was interested and trying my best to communicate.

Besides learning a language also the adoption of cultural habits helped in
gaining the trust of people. Living in a village helped me enormously to adopt
such habits and to closely observe ordinary people and to get to know their
habits. It made me feel more at home, even when I was working in other
villages. Informants often expected that I was living in Urgench, the provincial capital and were amazed when they found out that I was also living in a
rural area. Often people did, however, not understand why I would stay in a
village, if I also had the opportunity of staying in the city; there is clear cultural understanding that if you are doing well you move to the centre.

Besides assuming the identity of a villager, in some situations I also used
other identities to gain trust or respect. Obviously I was always a foreigner. I
stressed this sometimes in order to play the ignorant and inquired about the
'obvious'. Also it seemed that people were more inclined to trust a foreigner
with particular sensitive information. In a similar way, in a few situations, I
stressed my project membership, and connected to that, my status as a diplomat[3]. This always helped to settle difficult questions related to research
permissions.

In encounters with engineers and water managers I often stressed my
background as an irrigation engineer. Both the identity issue and my basic
technical knowledge on water issues were beneficial to be able to talk about
practicalities and understand the technicalities of their problems.

## Conversational techniques

In situations where I noticed that informants were hesitant to talk about a
specific topic, or when I was aware that the topic was sensitive to talk about,
I often introduced it with reference to what I had heard before from other
people in other situations. This obviously helped to break people's fear of
talking about the topic, presumably with the logic that if others talk about the

topic they can just as well also talk about it. Moreover, as it showed that I had more than one source for the information, they would run less risk of being exposed as the source of a particular view or comments. I was aware that my strategy might just as well distort the answer, as it would be easy for an informant to 'fool' me by giving an answer in line with the idea that I had sketched. I put up with this risk as otherwise people often would not talk about the specific subject at all.

In the beginning of the research I made use of a dictaphone a few times as some people had suggested to me that especially state officials would feel taken more seriously. I had the strong impression that it made informants feel uncomfortable. The difference between what was said during the running of the tape and what was said once the recording was stopped, however, gave interesting circumstantial information.

In the field I only made use of a small notebook in which I quickly noted down the most important information. In the beginning I was often making notes during the interview, but in later stages of the research I did it more and more directly after finalising the conversation. The taking of notes during the talking obstructed the flow of the interview, partly because of the distractions and time needed for that and partly because people would be constantly aware that I was observing and writing down everything they said. Though moving the note taking somewhat out of sight of the interviewees I was not secretive about it. I always let people know that I was taking notes and using the information they gave me. Postponing the jotting down frequently led to the loss of some details and accuracy, but in my assessment the advantages were larger than the disadvantages.

In principle I tried to ask open questions and let people free in their responses. Often I did not get direct answers to my questions and it was difficult to assess whether people were on purpose avoiding the question or whether they wrongly understood the question[4]. I usually tried to clarify the question by phrasing it differently. Or when that also did not work sometimes suggested a few answers to choose from. Suggesting answers certainly made it easier to understand the question, but frequently I had the impression that people were trying to give socially desirable answers. In situations where I had the strong impression that people were purposefully sketching me a situation or argument that seemed highly unlikely to me, I sometimes suggested them my contrary opinion on the case or told them about earlier observations that refuted the presented picture. In only very few cases this led to a change of the story, so methodologically it was not very effective. This definitely bears the risk of pushing people into a subordinate or defensive position, which increases the risks of socially desirable and evasive answers. On the other hand, doing this did make clear that I did not just accept everything and that even though generally taking an attitude of listening and asking for clarifications, there were limits. I had the impression that in the long run this had the positive effect that some informants took me more seriously.

### *Moving between observation and theory*

Being able to move between theory and observation (see sections 2 and 3) requires the production, storage and analysis of observations in a particular way. Taking field notes and working with them is at the centre of the qualitative research process. In the first place it is the storage of facts and observations, described as accurately and precisely as possible. But one also "tries to get 'behind' the observations, [...] they are not taken at their face value" (Alasuutari, 1995: 41). Therefore also the contextual information and interpretations are added to the field notes. It is, however, important to keep these interpretations clearly distinguished from the observations.

> "The method is without doubt poor if it does not enable the data to surprise, if the empirical analysis cannot even in theory give the researcher feedback that shows the need for improvements in the hypothesis or the design" (ibid.: 42).

This 'surprising' can be achieved by writing out the observations in detail, without jumping to interpretations. Doing this consistently takes time, effort and considerable length of writing, but in the end is rewarding as the field notes can be used as 'raw material' in which also new things can be discovered, on top of what was seen and interpreted at the moment of writing. Distinguishing between direct observations, contextual information (for instance from earlier fieldwork) and interpretations mostly shows from the writing style, but for clarity I often added straight brackets and accolades around the latter two.

The process of oscillating between theory and empirical material continued during the writing process. New codes and interpretations were added to the field notes, while existing literature was read or re-read with the objective to apply them to situations encountered in the field. Ideas were checked with the empirical material by searching through the field notes for good examples and situations that could refute or refine the arguments.

## Two problems

The described methodology explicitly took into account the specific difficulties in rural Uzbekistan. In spite of this there are two problematic effects with regard to the validity of the results. Firstly there was the problem with cross-checking of data though different ways of triangulation. And secondly there are biases in the research due to certain groups of actors being over-represented.

The main problem with cross-checking data was the sensitivity of the information that people gave me. This could partly be overcome through working at multiple sites and comparing the principles of individual cases with each other rather than fully cross-checking the details of reported stories. Also the mixed-method triangulation helped in getting different sorts of (contextual) information. However, also in mixed method triangulation problems were encountered. Especially the lack of reliable official data was problematic. Many researchers in Uzbekistan have reported to receive conflicting data sets as well as the suspicion of 'doctored' data (Mueller, 2006; Conrad, 2006; Wegerich, 2005). I am especially aware of examples of economic data and water discharge data, but this is probably connected to the sphere in which our project is active.

The use of such secondary data was limited and instead I relied as much as possible on data that could be cross-checked with own observations in the field. With regard to discharge data, which I did use on a wider scale, I used data from the lowest level in the state hierarchy. I camera copied this sort of data at the offices where the data was actually collected. Furthermore, the people collecting the data were able to explain me in detail the procedures by which they collected and administrated data. Also such data was not of perfect quality, as these measurements were not always accurately done and in a number of cases not done at all. But at least of this data I could be pretty sure that it was not doctored to show lower water use or more equal patterns of water use between districts. Such doctoring was sometimes expected on basis of other research results, especially Conrad (2006) and Wegerich (2005).

The second problem is that of over representation of some views over others. People that have an informed insight on the inner workings of WUAs or the state organisation at district level are sparse. The people that also feel free to talk about these sensitive topics are even rarer. It soon turned out many of the key informants are in a particular group, which leads to specific biases – in general they are male, they are relatively wealthy, well-educated and connected to the local elites, and many of them had a function in the state system. Often they had a close relative or other patron at a powerful position, which apparently gave them the ability to freely talk about such issues. Besides that it was difficult to cross-check the stories that they told (see above). Also, without an exception they represented the views of the *fermers*. Ordinary *dekhans* often had no insight in the processes under research, nor would they have felt free to share it with me. In the absence of a critical peasant or farmers' movement in Uzbekistan it is difficult to generate ideas and critiques informed by their insights.

## 5. Conclusion

My experience with approaching a politically sensitive topic through an integrated approach and mixed methods triangulations results in a number of recommendations. First of all, a bottom-up approach that starts with living in a village, learning Uzbek and slowly building-up rapport with ordinary people has proved effective – it seems unnecessary to start with the authorities and work one's way down to field level. This is, however, only possible when permissions have been pre-arranged, for instance through working in a large research project. Still, it requires sensitivity in working with people in official positions. In my experience it is more useful to once in a while be sent around to places and people that tell the official story rather than to be seen as somebody working outside the set boundaries. In the latter case people do not feel free to talk and if they do they might bring themselves into trouble. Similarly, I never explicitly sought to research illegal activities. Though at some point paddy cultivation did have my attention, I did not look into the issue because of its illegality, but because of its strong influence on water distribution.

The use of a professional identity proved very useful if I compare my work with that of some colleagues, who had difficulties in finding a credible excuse to 'hang around' in the field. Not only the identity, but also practical and thorough technical knowledge of the research topic are an enormous advantage. This also helps to position oneself in action situations, where interviews can be combined with direct observations. In general it is a big advantage to be able to do direct observations compared to just interviews, as people tend to be more at ease when engaged in activities, it often leads to practical questions that also have a deeper meaning and observation of the activities also lead to new insights.

Above all, the mixed method triangulation with a retroduction or riddle solving approach has proved particularly useful in a problematic research context. It provides the opportunity for trying a variety of methods and assessing the practical advantages and disadvantages of each in the particular setting. This flexibility is necessary to be able to respond to the many difficulties encountered in the field. Also the approach was apt to be deployed in a situation where only very little was known on the research topic. The approach allowed for theory development and restructuring rather than for theory testing. In the sketched environment it will be difficult to move towards reliable quantification of the identified processes. However, there are good opportunities for theory refinement and reconstruction.

Just as some topics were avoided during fieldwork, also in the written material (papers and dissertation) some topics as well as some concrete references will be omitted. Partly this is as a result of the field material lacking for it, and partly because it might threaten my informants or the ZEF/UNESCO project of which this research is part. Such self-censorship is not strange to Uzbek media and society (Shafer and Freedman, 2003). For me, however, it was a new phenomenon. Within the ZEF/UNESCO project we have had recurring discussions on what we can and what we cannot write in order not create threats to the continuation of the project and/or the personal safety of the people that we work with. It is a sad thing that this must be an issue and it is a compromise to academic standards that even we have to conclude that in some ways we have to restrict ourselves. To me the bottom line is that it should at least be possible to publicly state that, in our own perception, we cannot write everything, i.e. we actively and consciously censor our work to keep it acceptable for the Uzbek government.

It may be clear that there are serious limitations to conducting social science research in Uzbekistan, yet with use of the approach discussed above the research has been able to gain access to issues and developments in Uzbek society that were unknown before. Among other things this research sheds light on state control in practice, socio-economic differentiation processes in agriculture, and the practice of new institutions that are implemented under influence of worldwide neo-liberal agendas (such as Water Users Associations and water pricing). These are valuable findings that may have their effect on research and implementation processes and eventually they might inform rural transformation processes and in that way benefit the people of Uzbekistan.

## Acknowledgements

This paper is based upon research conducted under the ZEF/BMBF/UNESCO project "Economic and Ecological restructuring of land and water use in Khorezm", funded by the German Federal Ministry of Education and Research (Project Number 0339970A). I want to thank Caleb Wall and Tommaso Trevisani for sharing their field experiences - it has very much helped me to develop this research methodology. Furthermore this paper has greatly benefited from reviews by Peter Mollinga, Claire Wilkinson and Charles Palmer.

## Notes

[1] Spoor (2006:2) criticised the ICG report for seemingly suggesting in this report "that if cotton is taken away all will be well with the region, which is a rather unfounded view. It (...) hides that the cotton crop can (with necessary and appropriate institutional reforms) become the engine of agro-industry led growth and development."

[2] Though there are contrasting views on the volume of economic extraction in recent years (compare for instance Mueller (2006) with World Bank (2005)), there is agreement on a downward trend.

[3] As researcher of the ZEF/UNESCO project I had an accreditation as diplomat that belonged to a UN-organisation.

[4] Possibly this was also under influence of sometimes precarious translations with field assistants whose English was sometimes far from perfect.

## References

Adams, L. L. (1999) 'The mascot researcher: identity, power, and knowledge in fieldwork.' *The Journal of Contemporary Ethnography* 28(4):331-363

Alasuutari, P. (1995) *Researching culture: qualitative method and cultural studies.* Sage Publications, London

Bolding, A. (2004) *In hot water: a study on sociotechnical intervention models and practices of water use in smallholder agriculture, Nyanyadzi catchment, Zimbabwe.* PhD Thesis, Wageningen University

Bryman, A. (2004) *Social research methods.* Oxford University Press, Oxford

Burawoy, M. (1998). The extended case method. *Sociological Theory* 16(1):4-33

Callon, M. (1991). 'Techno-economic networks and irreversibility.' In: J. Law (ed.) *A sociology of monsters? Essays on power, technology and domination.* Sociological Review Monograph 38. Routledge, London, pp 132– 161

Conrad, C. (2006) *Fernerkundungsbasierte Modellierung und hydrologische Messungen zur Analyse und Bewertung der landwirtschaftlichen Wassernutzung in der Region Khorezm (Usbekistan).* PhD Thesis, Bonn University, Center for Development Research (ZEF)

Downward, P. and A. Mearman (2007) 'Retroduction as mixed-methods triangulation in economic research: reorienting economics into social science.' *Cambridge Journal of Economics* 31(1):77-99

Glaser, B.G. and A. Strauss (1967) *The discovery of grounded theory: strategies for qualitative research.* Aldine, New York

Hirschman, A.O. (1970) *Exit, voice and loyalty, responses to decline in firms, organizations and states.* Harvard University Press Cambridge, MA

ICG (2005) 'The curse of cotton: Central Asia's destructive monoculture.' *Asia Report* 93, International Crisis Group

Kandiyoti, D. (1999) Poverty in transition: an ethnographic critique of household surveys in post-Soviet Central Asia. *Development and Change* 30:499-524

Latour, B. (1991) 'Technology is Society Made Durable.' In J. Law (Ed.) *A Sociology of Monsters? Essays on Power, Technology and Domination.* Sociological Review Monograph 38, Routledge, London, pp 103– 131

Mueller, M. (2006) *A general equilibrium approach to modeling water and land use reforms in Uzbekistan.* PhD Thesis, Bonn University, Center for Development Research (ZEF)

Sayer, A. (1992) *Method in social science: a realist approach.* Routledge, London and New York

Sayer, A. (2000) *Realism and social science.* Sage, London

Shafer, R and E. Freedman (2003) Obstacles to the professionalization of mass media in Post-Soviet Central Asia: a case study of Uzbekistan. *Journalism Studies* 4(1):91–103

Spoor, M. (2006) *Cotton in Central Asia: 'curse' or 'foundation for development'?* Paper presented at the International Conference "The Cotton Sector in Central Asia", Centre of Contemporary Central Asia and the Caucasus, SOAS, University of London, 3-4 November 2005

Thompson, B (2007) http://www.cuyamaca.net/bruce.thompson/Fallacies/intro_fallacies.asp (03/05/2007).

Van der Zaag, P., and Bolding, A., and E. Manzungu (2001) 'Water networks and the actor: The case of the Save River catchment, Zimbabwe.' In: P. Hebinck and G.Verschoor (eds.) *Resonances and dissonances in development: actors, networks and cultural repertoires.* Royal Van Gorcum, The Netherlands, pp 257-279

Veldwisch, G.J.A., A. Bolding and P. Wester (forthcoming - 2007) 'Sand in the engine: The travails of an irrigated rice scheme in the Bwanje Valley, Malawi.' *Journal of Development Studies*

Wall, C.R.L. and J. Overton (2006) 'Unethical ethics?: applying research ethics in Uzbekistan.' *Development in Practice* 16(1):62-67

Wegerich, K. (2005),Wasserverteilung im Flusseinzugsgebiet des Amudarja. Offene und verdeckte Probleme – heute und in der Zukunft.' In: S. Neubert, W. Scheumann, A. van Edig and W. Huppert (eds.) *Integriertes Wasserressourcen-Management (IWRM): Ein Konzept in die Praxis überführen.* Nomos-Verlag, pp 201-215

World Bank (2005) *Cotton taxation in Uzbekistan: opportunities for reform.* World Bank, Washington, DC